**Orthogonal
Town Planning
in Antiquity**

The MIT Press   Cambridge, Massachusetts, and London, England

**Orthogonal
Town Planning
in Antiquity**

Ferdinando Castagnoli

Originally published in Rome by
De Luca Editore under the auspices of
the Institute of Ancient Topography of
the University of Rome

Original title:
Ippodamo di Mileto e l'Urbanistica
a Pianta Ortogonale
Translated from the Italian
by Victor Caliandro
English translation Copyright © 1971
by The Massachusetts Institute of
Technology

This book was designed
by Lauri Rosser
It was set in Baskerville
by Wolf Composition Company, Inc.
printed on Oxford Sheerwhite
Opaque, 70 lb.
by Halliday Lithograph Corp.
and bound in Interlaken AV1-819 Gray
by Van Rees Book Binding Corp.
in the United States of America

ISBN 0 262 03042 X (hardcover)

Library of Congress
catalog card number: 70–148975

Many cities of the Greek and Roman world are based on an extremely regular plan derived from a rectangular grid of streets. The orthogonal scheme of street alignment was first observed, particularly by Promis,[1] in the Roman cities of northern Italy. These discoveries quickly became part of the study of Roman surveying, which shortly before the work of Promis had been well analyzed in the writings of the *gromatici* (land surveyors) and which in his time were being encountered in the remaining traces of the centuriation. These cities of northern Italy were Roman, and the doctrines of the *gromatici* were reminiscent of the Etruscan contribution to Roman culture. Nissen,[2] however, believed that late republican scholarship was responsible for the attribution to Etruria and that the delimitation was actually of ancient Italic origin. It was he who instigated research into like forms and repeated motifs as a means of tracing a single ethnic line.

The validity of these concepts was seemingly confirmed when, shortly afterward, studies of the terremare were begun. Their regularly planned layouts were considered the prototypes of Roman military camps. These ideas, which by this time had found general acceptance, were in particular endorsed by Helbig;[3] they had been proposed originally by Chierici.[4] Correcting his earlier viewpoint, Nissen[5] later formulated a different view of the problem, affirming an identity between the Greek and the Italian towns and a common center of origin in the Orient (Babylon or Egypt). He hypothesized that the development of the Italian town depended upon Carthage as a bridge, and recognized the importance of the colonies in the development of the uniform town plan.

At the same time the research being carried on by Beloch on the cities of Campania greatly increased the store of concrete data.[6] As early as 1878 he pointed to these Greek examples, especially Naples, to counter "Italicist" tendencies. However, he made no statement in regard to the general problem of origins and relations, whether the Greek and Italian plans were independent, or if the Italics learned their system from the Greek plans and the Greeks from the Orient. Through the largely philological research on Hippodamus of Miletus[7] the value of the Greek

[1] C. Promis, *Le antichità di Aosta*, Turin 1862, p. 139, and *Storia dell'antica Torino*, Turin 1869.
[2] H. Nissen, *Templum*, Berlin 1869, p. 9, 97.
[3] W. Helbig, *Die Italiker in der Poebene*, Leipzig 1879, p. 61.
[4] G. Chierici, *Le antichità preromane della provincia di Reggio nell'Emilia*, Reggio 1871.
[5] H. Nissen, *Pompeianische Studien*, Leipzig 1877, p. 583, also *Orientation I*, Berlin 1906, p. 79.
[6] J. Beloch, *Bull. Inst.* 1877, p. 9.
[7] See references in Chapter 3, note 1.

influence was being established. However, the importance of Hippodamus's work, though widely discussed, was limited mainly to that of a theoretical formulation of principles.

The problem again shifted when Brizio advanced the hypothesis that the Etruscans learned the art of city planning directly from the Orient.[8] The problem thus became tied to that of Etruscan origins. On one side were the adherents to the theory of continuity between the terremare, villanovian Bologna, the Etruscan cities, the "Roma Quadrata" of the Palatine Hill, and the Roman colonies and encampments and the theory of Etruscan–Roman scholarship that this entailed. Their position is maintained in the more comprehensive studies, such as those by Haverfield, von Gerkan, Cultrera, and Lehmann–Hartleben. Täubler even went so far as to discern a terremare plan on the Palatine and on this evidence to affirm the derivation of the Latins from the inhabitants of the terremare.

In contrast to these positions are the adherents to the theory of the Eastern origins of delimitation, among whom are Lavedan, Ducati, and with particular commitment Patroni.

Separate from either of these considerations is Thulin's theory, which postulates that the Etruscans gained knowledge of the uniform grid plan from the Greeks.[9]

The question of the grid plan was approached for the first time in a general study by Haverfield.[10] To him the source of Greek urbanism lay in the Orient. However, he established that the Italian cities originated independently, recognizing in them the unique characteristic of the central street crossing, a feature absent from Greek plans. He sees the terremare, with Marzabotto, Pompeii, Norba, and Modena, as part of a continuity, while the later colonies are thought to be a fusion of the Italic and Hellenistic plans.

These concepts were further developed by von Gerkan in his fundamental work on ancient city planning,[11] in which the problem of the orthogonally patterned city occupies a prominent place. He further defines the characteristics of the Italic plan as based upon the axial system of two principal streets and compares this with the main *cardine* and *decumanus* of the centuriation.

[8] E. Brizio, *Mon. Lincei I*, 1890, p. 293.
[9] C. O. Thulin, *Die etruskische Disciplin III*, in *Die Ritualbücher, Göteborgs Högskolas Årsskrift* 1909, p. 37.
[10] F. Haverfield, *Ancient Town-Planning*, Oxford 1913.
[11] A. von Gerkan, *Griechische Städteanlagen*, Berlin and Leipzig 1924. See also *Röm. Mitt.* 58, 1943, p. 170.

This system then includes the terremare, Rome, and Pompeii. The Greeks did not employ this system of axes, nor did they attach a religious significance to the plan. As to the supposed relations between the Greek and Oriental city, von Gerkan notes that nowhere in the Orient can one find a rectangular grid; axial planning was employed in individual buildings only. Thus he sees the grid system as a natural development of the Greek colonies and Hippodamus, who lived in the fifth century B.C., as the theorizer of a much more ancient system.

Opposing these views, Cultrera saw precedents of the "Hippodamean" type throughout the Orient and in Crete.[12] He therefore proposed to attribute to Hippodamus not the orthogonal grid plan but a plan distinguished by its exploitation of scenographic qualities of the landscape. Whether the plan is rectangular or semicircular with radial divisions is not important. Cultrera further endorsed the current theory of a single Italic tradition, in which he included Fondi and Marzabotto in addition to the terremare and Roma Quadrata, by denying both the ties with Greece and the Etruscan introduction of Oriental prototypes. He resolved the problem of Soluntum by claiming a Phoenician origin for it and probably also for Selinus, though at a later date. He saw the cities of Campania as belonging to a region occupied by non-Greek peoples, including Etruscans.

Under the title "Städtebau" in the *Realencyclopaedie*,[13] the uniform grid plan is discussed both in the section on Greece by E. Fabricius and in that on Italy by K. Lehmann-Hartleben. The latter sees a clear connection between terremare and Etruscan cities and finds a surprising similarity in the plans of terremare and Marzabotto (with no similarity to Greek cities). Reversing Thulin's position on Campania, Lehmann-Hartleben maintains that in the new settlements the Greeks copied the examples of Capua and other Etruscan cities. Selinus then could be a late imitation dated 409 B.C.

The positions of Lavedan[14] and Ducati[15] are close, stemming from the theory of a single origin, the Orient, for both the Etruscan line (consistent with the theory of immigration) and the Greek. Concerning Greece, Ducati recalls the Milesian origin of Hippodamus and also proposes the possibility of mediation by the

[12] G. Cultrera "Architettura ippodamea. Contributo alla storia dell'edilizia nell'antichità," *Mem. Lincei* 5, 17, 1923, p. 361.
[13] Pauly–Wissowa, *Realencyclopaedie* III A, c. 1982, column 2016.
[14] P. Lavedan, *Histoire de l'urbanisme*, Paris 1926, p. 103, 141.
[15] P. Ducati, *Storia dell'arte etrusca I*, Florence 1927, p. 374.

Phoenicians. He calls attention to the importance of Soluntum for the Phoenicians.

With this, Pace[16] was drawn into the argument and pointed out that other regular plans are older yet. He concluded that such plans are inspired by the original requirements for order in new settlements.

Leaving aside the question of orthogonality, Tritsch[17] makes a distinction between the Greek cities, modeled after the Mycenean, and the terremare and Etruscan cities which came close to the centralized Oriental type.

New light was thrown on the issue when first Patroni and then Säflund proved that the reconstruction of a regular oriented plan in the case of the terremare was wrong. The ensuing discussion between Rose, sustaining the theory of continuity between terremare and Etruria, and Patroni, opposed to that view, was especially important.[18] Having demolished the theory of Italic origins, Patroni called the art of planning Etruscan,[19] directly introduced by them from the Orient, and he specifically considered ancient Mesopotamia as the place of origin. Of the Etruscan examples he cited Vetulonia, Marzabotto, and Pompeii. Greek planning, he thought, was also derived from the Orient but as a debased art having lost its religious significance, which the Etruscans maintained. Von Gerkan[20] replied to Patroni that in the western parts of Asia Minor, where the Etruscans were supposed to have originated, as well as in Mesopotamia, there are no cities truly laid out on the system of *cardine* and *decumanus*.

Martin credits the grid plan to Oriental origins, the nature of which remains to be determined, and considers the Greek colonies of the seventh and sixth centuries B.C. to be the first important phase of its development.[21]

[16] B. Pace, *Arte e civiltà della Sicilia antica II*, Milan 1938, p. 367. M. Zocca, in particular, stresses the universality of the rectangular layout. See his "Origini ed evoluzione degli schemi urbanistici," *Palladio*, N.S. 3, 1953, p. 21.
[17] F. Tritsch, "Die Stadtbildungen des Altertums und die griechische Polis," *Klio*, 22, 1928, pp. 1–83.
[18] H. J. Rose, "The Inauguration of Numa," *J. Roman Studies* 13, 1923, p. 82, and *Primitive Culture in Italy*, London 1926, p. 27. G. Patroni, "Voci e concetti classici arbitrariamente applicati alle terremare," *Athenaeum*, N.S. 8, 1930, p. 425; and Rose, "De templi romani origine," *ibid.* 9, 1931, p. 3.
[19] See especially "Vetulonia, Pompei e la storia," *Studi Etruschi* 15, 1941, p. 109.
[20] *Röm. Mitt.* 58, 1943, p. 170.
[21] R. Martin, "Recherches sur l'agora grecque," *Bibl. Ec. Française* 174, Paris 1951, p. 350. According to S. Parnicki–Pudelko, "Z problemow planowania miast w starozytnej Grecji," *Archeologia* 4, 1950–51, p. 27, Oriental influences accompany the evolution of the master plan from Tyrins to Miletus.

The discussion of city plans has also dealt with the quadripartite circular plan, of which Roma Quadrata is supposed to be an example. The origins of such a plan are either in the north, as claimed by W. Müller,[22] or in the Orient, according to Dornseiff.[23]

The general lines of the problem have been laid down recently by Boethius, by Brown, and by Ward Perkins. Boethius considers the time around 500 B.C. as crucial, a date to which he attributes Selinus, Paestum, and Marzabotto.[24] He concludes that there was definite Greek influence in Italy, or rather that in a common cultural environment Italy developed older rules of city planning. Brown points out the ties between the Etruscan cities and the older Roman colonies, between Marzabotto and Cosa, but leaves open the question of the ties to similar Greek cities in Campania.[25] By emphasizing the functions of Roman cities rather that their origins, Ward Perkins highlights the historical conditions that gave rise to the cities: military order and the imitation of the Etruscan city (which in turn developed with dependence on Greece).[26] He discounts the theories of the erudite Romans.

The paucity of knowledge of town plans creates major difficulties. Temples and tombs are unearthed, but urban complexes are not often excavated—or at least their disposition and measurements are not as fully explored as they should be. Furthermore, the existing documentation of plans is generally inaccurate, thereby giving conclusions a provisional character. In the present work some plans are derived from aerial photographs. It is scarcely necessary to caution that some of these have only a superficial value.

If we rule out the thesis of terremare and Italic origins, the study of grid planning today presents the following interdependent concerns:

Must we consider as a whole all the entire urban planning of the

[22] W. Müller, *Kreis und Kreuz*, Berlin 1938.
[23] F. Dornseiff, "Roma Quadrata," *Rhein. Mus.* 88, 1939, p. 192.
[24] A. Boethius, "Roman and Greek Town Architecture," *Göteborgs Högskolas Årsskrift* 54, 1948:3, p. 7; "Die hellenisierte italische Stadt der römischen Republik," *Acta Instituti Athen. Regni Sueciae* 4⁰, II, 1953, p. 177.
[25] F. E. Brown, "Cosa I," *Mem. Amer. Acad.* 20, 1951, p. 107 and especially n. 101.
[26] J. B. Ward Perkins, "The Early Development of Roman Town-Planning," mimeographed paper presented at the Second International Congress of Classical Studies in Copenhagen, August 1954; also "Early Roman Towns in Italy," *Town Planning Review* 26, 1955, p. 127.

Etruscans and Romans as a single unit? That is, is there a system that will embrace not only the Roman colony from the fourth century on, but also the Etruscan cities of Capua, Marzabotto, and Pompeii, not to mention Roma Quadrata, the doctrines of the *gromatici*, and the theory of delimitation?

What are the relations between these cities and the Greek city? Are they interdependent? Are the Etruscans emulators of the Greeks, or vice versa? The theory which maintains the Greek origins of the grid must account for the plan of Etruscan Capua, while the Etruscan-origin theory must put Selinus at a later date.

If the Hippodamean city came before Hippodamus himself, must one think of him, as is usual, as a theorist enjoying a borrowed reputation, or must one consider his work under a different light —as scenographic urbanism, for example?

Finally, must the Oriental influence be understood in a generic way? Or is it a direct source, as is thought by those who maintain the Oriental origins of the Etruscans, who emphasize the Milesian origins of Hippodamus, and who attribute Selinus and Soluntum to the Carthaginians?

Chapter 1

Cities of the Sixth and Fifth Centuries B.C.

Orthogonal Intersections

Olbia

Selinus

Grid planning systems based upon the orthogonal intersection of roads have been recorded since the end of the sixth century B.C.

At Olbia, a colony of Miletus on the Black Sea, Russian excavations have revealed a grid plan with a celestial orientation in the center of the upper city, apparently dating from the end of the sixth century. The city was rebuilt at that time after a fire.[1]

At the other end of the Greek world, at Selinus, we find the same system (Fig. 1). Indeed, the acropolis of Selinus is one of the crucial points for the investigation of regular city planning. If as early as the sixth century we find such a complete and perfect example, we do not know what innovations we must credit to Hippodamus, who lived in the fifth. Like Roman plans, the plan of Selinus is characterized by the orthogonal intersection of two major axes (the north–south axis is 9 meters wide). Further subdivisions create blocks, probably rectangular in shape, whose short side faces the *decumanus*. This side measures 28.1 to 29.95 meters, so apparently a 100-foot module was used as a base. The roads vary in width between 3.60 and 3.95 meters. This is obviously the *per strigas* subdivision that was common in the Greek cities of the fifth century, as will be seen later.

In attempting to explain the odd fact that such a plan should have appeared at such an early date, many scholars have sought its source among the works of the Phoenicians, in spite of the fact that neither Carthage nor any other Phoenician city shows any precedent for the grid plan at that time. To avoid assigning the plan to an era preceding Hippodamus, Fougères[2] among others attributes the present plan of Selinus to the period of reconstruction after 409 B.C.[3] Yet excavations by Gabrici[4] have revealed that the acropolis of Selinus was already being laid out along two major axes at the end of the sixth century. Not until the fourth century, however, was the acropolis subdivided into rectangular blocks. This happened during the decline of the city, when the acropolis became a residential sector. It is hoped that further excavations will clarify the chronological order of the plan of the acropolis.[5] At present it seems that we can do no more than confirm that a system of two major intersecting axes has existed since the sixth century. Beside being logical from the point of view of communications, as noted by Gabrici, this plan

[1] Pauly–Wissowa, *Realencyclopaedie* 17, c. 2416.
[2] G. Fougères and J. Hulot, *Sélinonte*, Paris 1910, p. 192.
[3] See also von Gerkan, *Griechische Städteanlagen*, p. 36.
[4] *Mon. Linc.* 33, 1930, c. 61.
[5] For more recent research on the fourth and fifth centuries B.C., see A. Di Vita, *Archeol. Class.* 5, 1953, p. 39.

10

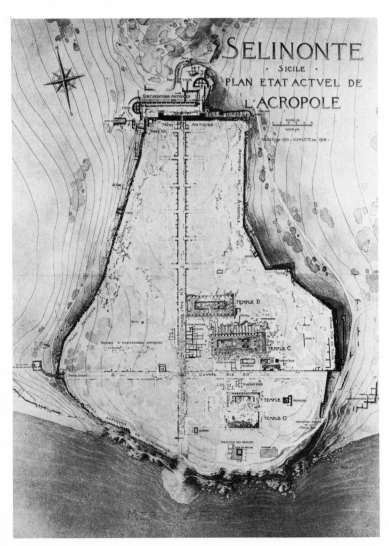

Figure 1 Selinus, acropolis (Fougères–Hulot).

is directly comparable to the layouts of other Greek cities (such as Olbia),[6] thereby making it unnecessary to take recourse to the theory of Italic influence, as Wycherley does.[7] This author has rightly observed, however, that in the sixth century Selinus did not yet have the complex grid plan found at Miletus and Olynthus.

Veii and other Etruscan Cities

In the Etruscan and Italic world, Veii is an important example of an intersection of two almost perfect orthogonal axes in the archaic residential sector of Piazza d'Armi.[8] The oldest part of Pompeii, going back to the sixth century, also has the axial scheme, whether Greek or Italic in origin. It may be that this same plan will be found in Etruscan centers explored by Cozza and Pasqui, especially Monterado between Montefiascone and Orvieto, because the gates of the enclosures, both circular and polygonal, seem to have been laid out by a celestial orientation.[9] The same form may have been employed at Cortona,[10] according to what can be deduced from the location of the city gates. (It is possible that the upper part of the ring of walls served only strategic purposes and did not correspond to the part of the city that was lived in.) Cortona's modern streets also suggest this plan, especially those which begin at Porta Castiglionese, Sant'Agostino, and at the now demolished Porta San Domenico, for they are straight and perpendicular to each other, and intersect at the urban center.[11]

Thus the oriented axial system is found in Greece as well as in Etruria. We cannot say, however, that it is specifically Etrusco–Italic. Furthermore, because it is a spontaneous method of organization, we can consider it to have developed independently in the two cultures.

Grid Plans
Miletus

Miletus was destroyed by the Persians in 494 B.C. and rebuilt either during the years after liberation (479)[12] or after 466,[13] becoming a well-known example of the grid plan (Fig. 2). The

---

[6] Uniform plan layouts were explored by Orsi at Monte Casale near the Palazzolo Acreide (a citadel dating back to the sixth century B.C.) and at Megara Iblea. See *Not. Scavi* 1925, p. 313.

[7] R. E. Wycherley, "Notes on Olynthus and Selinus," *Amer. J. Archeology* 55, 1951, p. 234.

[8] E. Stefani, *Mon. Lincei* 40, 1944, c. 211, figure 19, c. 228.

[9] *Mon. Lincei* 4, 1894, column 43.

[10] This can be compared to the map in the Touring Club Italiano guide.

[11] The imposing wall in *opus quadratum* (more than 40 meters) under the Palazzo della Cassa di Risparmio and under the Palazzo Pretorio is not oriented as shown by A. Neppi-Modona in *Cortona etrusca e romana*, Florence 1925, p. 50, but is perfectly aligned with the streets mentioned in the text. This is obvious from the fact that the sides of the two Palazzi mentioned are based on the wall.

[12] A. von Gerkan, *Milet* I, ch. 8, p. 120.

[13] Meyer in Pauly-Wissowa, *Realencyclopaedie* 25, c. 1633.

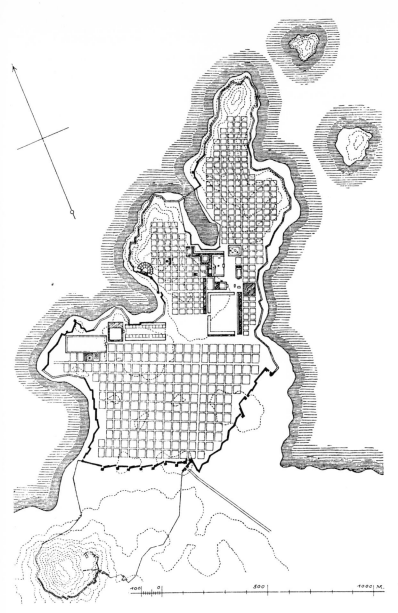

Figure 2 Miletus (von Gerkan).

13

plan, as reconstructed by Wiegand and von Gerkan,[14] presents two similar but distinct grid systems, developed successively, within which are set the largest buildings. The average city block measures 29.50 by 51.60 meters, or about 100 by 175 feet. Later developments may account for further longitudinal subdivisions. Two streets, wider than most (7.50 meters) and at right angles to each other, are to be found in the southern section of the city. The reconstruction is conjectural, however, since it is based on incomplete data.[15] The long sides of the blocks could have been much longer yet, while the short sides could have been arranged on wide lengthwise streets (one of which, leading to the Gate of the Lions, is known with certainty). Such a layout would be even more similar to that of the cities we are about to examine. In fact, such cities are characterized by a pattern of elongated blocks and by the greater importance of the lengthwise axes (more continuous and usually wider) on which the short sides of the blocks are established. In other words, the emphasis is on longitudinal strips, which are then subdivided into transverse blocks in a manner analogous to the system known to Roman surveyors as *per strigas*.

Olynthus

Olynthus,[16] founded in 432 B.C. and destroyed in 348, is a city of this type (Fig. 3). "Avenues" between 5 and 7 meters wide run north–south, complemented by perpendicular "streets" about 5 meters wide (Fig. 4). The resulting blocks[17] are 35.00 or 35.40 meters wide and about 86.34 meters long (120 by 300 feet), a width-to-length ratio of 1:2.5.

Rhodes

Rhodes follows the same scheme (Fig. 5). Many ancient authors have written of this city. The most reliable deduction about it, however, comes from the epithet θεατροειδής, found twice in Diodorus (XIX, 45; XX, 83). From this it has been inferred, by Hermann, Erdmann, and Cultrera, especially, that the city was patterned on a semicircular plan articulated by a system of radial streets.[18] This conclusion is important since, according to Strabo (XIV, 654), Rhodes was planned by the same architect who laid out Piraeus, namely Hippodamus.

Kondis's partial reconstruction of the city plan has been very

[14] T. Wiegand, *Achter Bericht, Abh. preuss. Ak. Wiss.* 1924, number 1; von Gerkan, *Griechische Städteanlagen*, p. 91, Table 6, and *Milet* I, 8, p. 106.
[15] Wiegand, *Achter Bericht*, p. 5, and von Gerkan, *Milet* I, 8, p. 111. Compare with Beilage III.
[16] D. M. Robinson and J. W. Graham, *Excavations at Olynthus* 8, Baltimore 1938, p. 29.
[17] These are divided along the long axis by an *ambitus* 1.40 meters wide.
[18] And also by W. B. Dinsmoor, *The Architecture of Ancient Greece*, London–New York 1950, p. 214 (compare with p. 263).

14

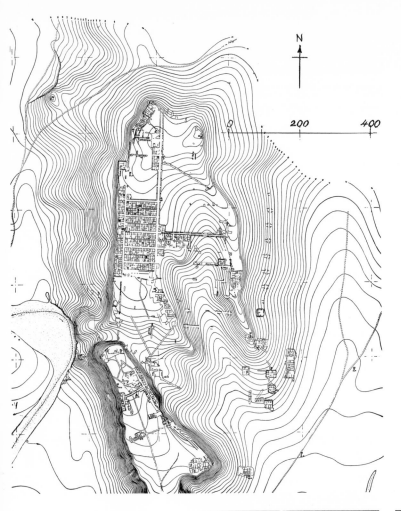

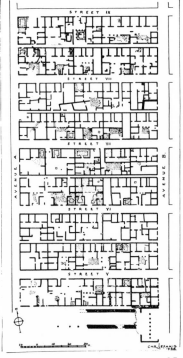

Figure 3 Olynthus (Robinson and Graham).

Figure 4 A quarter of Olynthus (Robinson and Graham).

15

Figure 5 Rhodes (Kondis).

important.[19] He has shown that Rhodes was patterned on orthogonal streets and was characterized, at least in some sectors, by subdivision *per strigas*. The resemblance to a theater obviously refers to the natural configuration of the terrain, which is bowl-shaped and slopes toward the port. Vitruvius (II, 8, 43) offers an explanation of this comparison in his description of Halicarnassus, which is often compared to the plan of Rhodes and is thought to be an outstanding example of a circular city: *is . . . locus est theatri curvaturae similis. Itaque in imo secundum portum forum est constitutum.* (The natural conformation is similar to the *cavea* of a theater. Thus the forum was disposed in the lowest part, along the port.) As we might expect, there are also references in Strabo, where the term θεατροειδής clearly refers to the physical setting.[20] Though incomplete, the restored plan shows what perhaps was an array of main streets grouped in the north–south direction. The distance between them, set by Kondis[21] at 100 feet, must have resulted in very long blocks. The plan corresponds perfectly to the description, attributed to Aristides (*Rhod.* 43, 6), of a city admirably subdivided, entirely regular and uniform (seeming to be one single city), with uninterrupted streets ((ἀγυιὰς ἐξ ἀρχῆς εἰς τέλος διηνεκεῖς ἥκιστα ἀξίας καλεῖσθαι στενωπούς).[22]

The founding of Rhodes dates from 408–407 B.C. Certainly reconstructions and enlargements have followed since, because of both the destruction and the growth of the city. It is possible, however, that a large section of the city (especially the center) corresponds to the original plan.

Aristotle (*Pol.* II, 1267b, 22), as well as several other sources, attributes the master plan of Piraeus to Hippodamus of Miletus. On the basis of a number of walls that intersect at right angles, it seems safe to say that the city had an orthogonal plan which must date from the days of Pericles (before 445).[23] A street 14 to 15 meters wide has also been confirmed. The reconstructions that have been made of the entire plan must remain conjectural, however.

Piraeus

Goodchild[24] had the good fortune to discover, from traces on an aerial photograph, a lost city near Bengasi which he identified

Euesperides

[19] I. D. Kondis, Συμβολὴ εἰς τὴν μελετὴν τῆς ῥυμοτομίας τῆς Ῥόδου Rhodes 1954. Before Kondis, A. Maiuri had made an important study, with a map at 1:25,000 showing the scheme of the ancient city, in his "Topografia monumentale di Rodi," *Clara Rhodos* 1, 1928, p. 44.
[20] Strabo 4, 179; 14, 656; 16, 73; for Massalia, Cnidus, and Jericho.
[21] The width of the streets is calculated at 2.5 and 4 meters.
[22] "Uninterrupted streets from beginning to end, which do not deserve to be called στενωποί."
[23] W. Judeich, *Topographie von Athen*, 2nd ed. Munich 1931, p. 430; p. 76, note 2.
[24] R. G. Goodchild, "A Devastated City Site," *Antiquity* 26, 1952, p. 208.

as the ancient Euesperides. Although the plan is not entirely uniform, it presents the usual subdivisions by two or three longitudinal axes intersected by much narrower perpendicular streets and thus forming a pattern of rectangular blocks (Fig. 6). These blocks vary in their dimensions; they measure about 44 meters (150 feet) in width in the southern part of the city and about 35 meters (120 feet), in the north, while the lengths vary between 80 and 130 meters in the southern blocks and are about 100 meters for the northern ones. As at Pompeii, such irregularities most probably result from successive expansions. Recent research shows that the life of the city extended from the fifth to the third centuries B.C. It was already in existence in 510 B.C.[25] and was to end its history by the middle of the third century, when Ptolemy III captured it and substituted for it the new city of Berenice.

Thurii

Important examples of the grid type of urban pattern are to be found chiefly in the West. Verification of the plan of Thurii, a city founded in 444–443 B.C.[26] on a plan by Hippodamus, would be of basic importance to these studies. We know of this plan through a description by Diodorus (XII, 10, 7): τήν τε πόλιν διελόμενοι κατὰ μὲν μῆκος εἰς τέτταρας πλατείας ..., κατὰ δὲ τὸ πλάτος διεῖλον εἰς τρεῖς πλατείας.[27] Thus the city is shown to have been patterned by orthogonal axes:[28] four in one direction and three in the other. It appears, however, that seven streets would be insufficient for a city the size of Thurii. Very likely the system of *cardines* and *decumani* was supplemented by a system of small streets. These are not πλατεῖαι but στενωποί, as at Hippodamean Rhodes.

The hypothesis of extra streets is not shared by von Gerkan,[29] who bases his argument on the passage of Diodorus immediately following the one just cited: τούτων δὲ τῶν στενωπῶν πεπληρωμένων ταῖς οἰκίαις ἡ πόλις ἐφαίνετο καλῶς κατεσκευάσθαι. This passage is frequently translated as, "And these streets being packed by dwellings ... " that is, the πλατεῖα and στενωπός apparently have lost their differences in meaning and simply mean urban streets.[30] Such a debasement is strange, since the terms were not synonymous[31] but had a precise difference of meaning in the urban theory of the time. (Their Latin counterparts *platea* and

[25] See Herodotus IV, 204.

[26] Regarding the questionable date of Thurii, see S. Accame, *Riv. Fil. Class.* 33, 1955, p. 164.

[27] "having divided the city lengthwise into four πλατεῖαι ... and widthwise into three πλατεῖαι."

[28] Some orthogonal elements are discernible in the abridged plan published in *Not. Scavi* 1879, Table V.

[29] *Griechische Städteanlagen*, p. 57.

[30] For example, C. H. Oldfather (Loeb).

[31] Στενωπός, meaning "narrow place" in Diodorus XXXI, p. 9, 2.

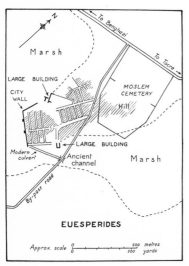

Figure 6 Euesperides (Goodchild).

18

angiportus are found in Vitruvius I, 6, 1; see note 12 of chapter 2.) It is probable that in place of τούτων δέ, used by Vogel because it is found in the most authoritative manuscript (Patmius, tenth or eleventh century), we should read instead ὑπὸ δὲ τούτων, given by the later manuscripts. Thus we can agree with C. Müller's translation: *Quumque vicos his interiectos domibus explevissent, urbs commode digesta et pulchre exaedificata videbatur.*[32]

Two other solutions are far less likely: to construe τούτων as a pronoun (relative to πλατεῖαι) dependent on στενωπῶν, and thus translate "these being the alleys of the streets (of the πλατεῖαι) packed with houses . . . " Alternately, we can consider ταῖς οἰκίαις to be a correction by the editors of τὰς οἰκίας in the manuscripts and can employ it as a relative accusative, noting that πληρόω is used with the genitive and not with the dative. We then translate as follows: "and these (the πλατεῖαι) being filled with στενωποί (completed by στενωποί) the city appeared well stocked with houses."

Through solutions of this type we avoid the improper use of terms in Diodorus and the mistake of ascribing only seven streets to an important city. In this description Diodorus speaks first of the general layout (main arteries which probably enclosed entire regions) and then of private construction—that is, the blind alleys whose function was to subdivide the city blocks rather than to establish pedestrian communication.

Subdivision *per strigas* is common to the next group of cities, known to us principally through excavations or through the carryover of their ancient plans into the layout of present cities. These are Agrigento, Pompeii, Herculaneum, Naples, Paestum, the acropolis of Selinus as arranged after 409 B.C., Capua, and Marzabotto.

Pirro Marconi includes the general layout of the city in his ingenious and penetrating study of Agrigento.[33] Marconi's opinion in regard to the Hippodamean city plan is that ". . . in many cities, including Agrigento, it is nearly impossible to find any principles of order; everything is fortuitously arranged, without a preconceived plan. In Agrigento especially, the abundance of available land made it even easier to leave matters to chance and individual initiative."[34] Marconi has examined the agglom-

Agrigento

---

[32]"Whenever they filled in the districts between these houses, the city seemed pleasantly arranged and beautifully built."

[33]P. Marconi, "Studi Agrigentini," in *Riv. Ist. Archeol. St. Arte* II, 1930, p. 7; and *Agrigento*, Firenze, 1929, p. 41, 116.

[34]*Agrigento*, p. 41, n. 1; cf. "Studi Agrigentini," p. 61.

erate of small dwellings in the northern sector, finding them disorganized and tightly packed, and noting the lack of any traces of urban organization. However, he does not exclude the possibility that other parts of the city were more uniformly organized, basing his theory on nonexistent evidence in Diodorus.[35] Marconi thinks that perhaps such sectors were to be found in the lower portions of the city, where Greek coins are often found.[36] The groups of houses of the Roman epoch found in this section give no sign of a possible new plan installed by the Romans.[37] He makes these statements notwithstanding the fact that the map on page 17 of his book *Agrigento* shows many rectilinear alignments of roads in the southern sector of the city. He even gives a reconstruction (on page 40) of the general layout of streets according to a plan that is entirely irregular.

Recently, near an unearthed block of Roman buildings (not far from San Nicola), a large and regularly planned neighborhood was excavated by Griffo,[38] which dated close to the end of the second century B.C. It is laid out on a large artery of more than 10 meters width, into which four *cardines* debouch, each between 4.75 and 5.35 meters wide and running the length of the excavation (200 m). The blocks are 36.55, 35.90, and 34.65 meters wide, respectively. This highly interesting excavation should be extended to give us a general picture of Agrigento's plan.

In the meantime we can develop an approximate reconstruction from studying aerial photographs, which show a group of small modern roads and terracing (Fig. 7).[39] In the central portions of the city there is a clear pattern of *cardines* enclosing blocks one actus wide and much elongated. Beneath the present state highway runs a *decumanus* more than 10 meters wide;[40] the one parallel to it probably ran some 300 meters to the south as at Paestum.[41] Another *decumanus* can be inferred from some tracks that would have passed through the agora. This, according to the

---

[35] In "Studi Agrigentini," p. 46, and elsewhere Marconi asserts that Diodorus XIII, 84, related that part of the city was of uniform pattern with comfortable and wide streets, and that part was irregular, with winding and dark streets through it (cf. Pace, *Arte e civiltà della Sicilia antica* II, p. 361); unfortunately, Diodorus does not speak directly of this, and the interpretation must then result from a misunderstanding of the Schubring–Tognazzo (p. 100) reading of this passage.

[36] *Agrigento*, p. 101; "Studi Agrigentini," p. 47.

[37] *Agrigento*, p. 117.

[38] G. Griffo, "Bilancio di cinque anni di scavo nelle provincie di Agrigento e Caltanissetta" (abstract from *Atti Accad. Scienze, Lettere e Arti di Agrigento*, III, 1953–54); and *Il quartiere ellenistico romano presso S. Nicola*, Agrigento, 1953.

[39] Note that the photograph is distorted along the edges.

[40] Griffo, *Il quartiere ellenistico*.

[41] The ruins in the eastern sector are part of the road which led to the western sector.

most generally accepted hypothesis,[42] was located near the
Olympieion and the Temple of Hercules. Finally, at the southern-
most part of the city layout are the remains of several houses to
the west of the Temple of Concord (Fig. 8).

The *decumani* run some 10 degrees north of east, though only
the Olympieion follows this orientation; the other temples face
directly east.

Thus a large part of Agrigento, the most important part, was
laid out in a uniform grid pattern. To the north, however, a
group of poorer dwellings has been found built into the hillside;
these follow no regular pattern.

When we consider a chronology for the layout, the area adjacent
to San Nicola must be attributed to the second century B.C. The
remains farther south go back to Roman times. Only the dwellings to the west of the Temple of Concord are attributed, by
Marconi,[43] to the fifth century. The Olympieion is almost
certainly a criterion in establishing a chronology of Agrigento,
since, as has been mentioned, it follows the orientation of the city.
The period during which the temple was built has been placed
between 480 and 460 B.C. (for the telamons and polychrome
tiles) and 450 to 440 (for the lion's head rainspouts and for
fragments of the pediment).[44] According to Diodorus (XIII, 82),
and Polybius (IX, 27) (but their testimony has been questioned),
the temple had not yet been completed by 406 B.C. In any case,
the Olympieion presupposes the existence of the city plan. This
means that the plan must be traced back to the founding of the
city in the first decades of the sixth century—the period to which
the walls have been ascribed—or more likely to the period
immediately following the battle of Imera (480 B.C.). It was after
this battle that the city assumed its monumental form. The major
temples date from that time, and we learn from Diodorus (XI,
25, 3) of the great numbers of prisoners taken in the battle who
were employed in quarrying the material that served to build
the temples and sewers.

Thus it is entirely possible that the most important sector of the
city could have been systematically planned and organized

---

[42] From historic references (Cicero, *Verr.* II, IV, 94; Livy XXVI, 40) we know
only that it was near the Temple of Hercules, perhaps not far from the gate
where the Romans entered the city in 208 B.C. (perhaps this was the porta
dell'Emporio). Concerning more recent excavations, which may be part of
the agora, see G. Griffo, *Ripresa degli scavi in Agrigento: Gli scavi nel settore
occidentale della zona archeologica*, Agrigento, 1953, p. 20.
[43] Marconi, *Agrigento*, p. 100.
[44] Marconi, *Riv. Ist. Archeol. St. Arte* I, 1929, p. 266.

Figure 7 Aerial view of Agrigento
(Istituto Geografico Mil.).

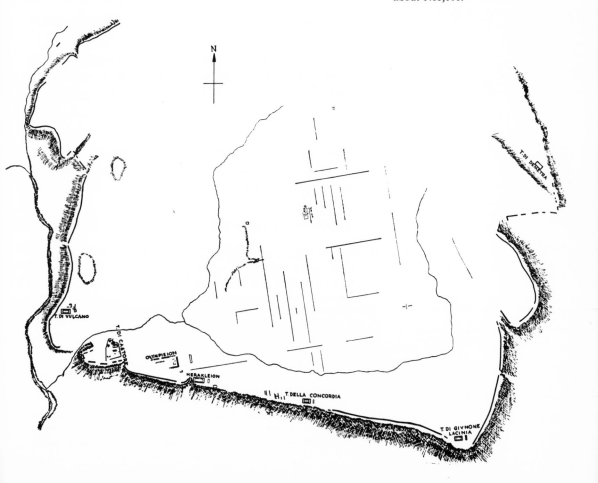

Figure 8 Agrigento, diagrammatically reconstructed. Scale is about 1:13,000.

during the period of its greatest splendor. Rather than thinking of master plans made during the renaissance of the city under Timoleon in 338 B.C. or during the Roman era, one can hypothesize that the second-century quarters were rebuilt on older foundations. Dwellings are more easily rebuilt than public buildings.

Pompeii

The plan of Pompeii has been the object of much research. From the beginning the uniformity and regular layout of the city were noted and attempts were made to trace the path of the *cardine* and *decumanus*. At first these were thought to be the Via di Nola and Via di Stabia. This theory was maintained into the time of Mau,[45] who supposed the central square to be the intersection of these roads,[46] as Sogliano still maintains.[47] Van Bezold, on the other hand, suggests that the Via di Mercurio with its southerly extension and the Via dell'Abbondanza correspond to the *cardine* and *decumanus*.[48]

The first positive step in understanding the plan was Haverfield's recognition of the original center of the city.[49] He believed that the southern sector around the Forum, whose plan is well marked and is independent of the remaining sectors, marks the first phase of the urban development of Pompeii.

This early city has been described often, especially by von Gerkan.[50] Its boundaries are clear for the most part: Vico dei Soprastanti, Via degli Augustali, Vicolo del Lupanare, and Via dei Teatri. The Foro Triangolare was probably outside, and the boundaries of the west side are questionable.[51] The principal axes were also clear; the Via della Marina with the first section of the Via dell'Abbondanza may be considered the original *decumanus*, while the Via delle Scuole, the Forum, and a section of street which perhaps was in the northern part of the present Forum make up the *cardine*.

The scheme is clearly an axial one, with intersection at the Forum.

[45] A. Mau, "La piazza centrale di Pompei," in *Bull. Inst.* 1875, p. 261.
[46] Mau also tried to reconstruct an accurate plan through the entire extent of the city and saw evidence of this in a column imbedded in a house.
[47] A. Sogliano, "Il Foro di Pompei," in *Mem. Lincei*, VI, I, 1925, p. 221; also "La fase etrusca di Pompei," in *Studi Etruschi* I, 1927, p. 173; *Pompei nel suo sviluppo storico. Pompei Preromana*, Roma, 1937, p. 40, 54.
[48] G. van Bezold, "Osservazioni sulla limitazione di Pompei," in *Bull. Inst.* 1880, p. 151 ff.
[49] *Ancient Town-Planning*, p. 63. Also F. von Duhn, *Pompeji, eine hellenistische Stadt*, 1st. ed., Leipzig, 1906, p. 24, reconstruction of a Greek city with the acropolis on the terrace of the Foro Triangulare.
[50] A. von Gerkan, *Der Stadtplan von Pompeji*, Berlin 1940.
[51] Up to the Porta Marina, according to F. Noack and K. Lehmann-Hartleben, *Baugeschichtliche Untersuchungen am Stadtrand von Pompeji*, Berlin and Leipzig, 1936, p. 1; countering these views, von Gerkan, *Stadtplan von Pompeji*, p. 22.

Yet several irregularities in the plan cannot be overlooked. The axis of the *decumanus* is broken at the temple of Apollo; the *cardine* is not perfectly orthogonal. According to von Gerkan, a gate should correspond to the extension of Vico Storto, and at 83 meters from the gate of the *cardine*, opposite the gate of Vico Storto, there should be yet another gate, since at that point there is evidence of a street (Vicolo del Gallo) even though it runs only inside the ancient city. This hypothesis of von Gerkan is less certain; it is more likely that there is a gate corresponding to the Vico delle Terme which would fall alongside the Temple of Apollo. The Vico delle Terme may follow the extension of the consular road.

The alignment of the Temple of Apollo, parallel with the *cardine*, is especially important. A wall built in the middle of the second century B.C.[52] to the north of the Forum, near the Capitolium, also runs parallel to it. The *decumanus* only briefly follows this orientation (Via della Marina); because of this, Sulze[53] falls back on the gratuitous hypothesis that the Via dell'Abbondanza may represent a later correction to the *decumanus* and that the original *decumanus*, following the alignment of Via della Marina may end north of the Terme Stabiane. One must realize, however, that in the ancient nucleus of Pompeii the axial system was not used as rigorously as in other cities.[54]

Some scholars claim that the growth and development of the entire city took place in one single phase. Others think that there were at least two successive phases: the first an extension to the north of the Forum, the second toward the east, terminating at the present boundaries of the city. Spano[55] maintains that these two successive periods of development were carried out under the Samnites, whereas the ancient nucleus of Pompeii was built by the Etruscans. However, Patroni[56] attributes Region VI, because of its regular pattern, to the Etruscans, who are thought to have settled in Pompeii during the sixth century B.C. and to have built a quarter *ex novo*. Attempts have been made to validate this theory through such arguments as the famous "Etruscan" column of Region VI and the supposedly Etruscan heraldry on

[52] Maiuri, *Not. Scavi*, 1942, p. 313.
[53] H. Sulze, "Der Decumanus Maximus des ältesten Pompeji," in *Forsch. und Forschr.*, 17, 1941, p. 377. Countering this is von Gerkan, *Röm. Mitt.* 58, 1943, p. 174. Cf. also H. Sulze, "Zum Stand der Forschung über die Städtebauliche Entwicklung Pompejis," in *Forsch. und Forschr.* 26, 1950, p. 33.
[54] From the imperfect axiality within the system is derived the irregular plan layout of several buildings (temple of Apollo, the building of Eumachia, and others).
[55] G. Spano, *La Campania Felice nelle età più remote. Pompei dalle origini alla fase ellenistica*, Napoli, 1941.
[56] G. Patroni, *Vetulonia, Pompei e la sua storia*, in *St. Etr.*, 15, 1941, p. 109.

the houses there.[57] According to Patroni's theory, Regions VII and VIII were built after Region VI, thereby reversing the commonly accepted sequence of Pompeii's development. The *cardine* then would be the Strada di Mercurio, while the Via di Nola would be the *decumanus*.

The complete and clearly defined plan of the original Pompeii around the Forum argues against Patroni's theory. Indeed, the uniformity of the general city plan outside the original nucleus contradicts the idea of a two-phase development—that is, a development of Region VI prior to that of Regions V, IX, and others. In short, the development of the entire urban fabric occurred in only two successive phases: the archaic nucleus and its extension to the present limits.

The principles governing the second phase of development were carefully studied by von Gerkan (Fig. 9),[58] who thought he recognized *Landstrassen* roads which at the time of the original Pompeii lay outside the city, on which the new city would be built. These roads were the Via di Mercurio (considered an external extension of the original *cardine*), Via di Nola (thought to be a major artery between Naples, Nola, Nocera, and Salerno) and Via di Stabia (a large road between Naples and Stabia).[59] Such heavily traveled roads would not have passed through the old Pompeii, which was autonomous. Along this preexisting layout the present city of Pompeii was thought to have developed.

Rather than counter von Gerkan's theory,[60] it is preferable to describe the physiognomy of greater Pompeii, that is of a city with a clear and unified pattern, having evolved with only such limitations as are imposed by the forms of the archaic nucleus. This relation to the old city adds interest to the wide variety of solutions that were to arise (Figs. 10 and 11).

The Via di Nola and the Via dell'Abbondanza are the longitudinal axes, the *decumani* that characterize Greek city plans. They subdivide the city into three strips of equal width. The Via

[57] See D. Folco Carozzi, *Rend. Ist. Lomb.*, 71, 1938, p. 566.
[58] The plan is reproduced in *Stadtplan*, Fig. 1, brought up to date in *Städteanlagen*, Fig. 15.
[59] Van Buren (*Class. Journal*, 15, 1919–20, p. 170, 404; see *Mem. Amer. Acad.*, 5, 1925, p. 106) thought the consular road, Via degli Augustali, and the southern section of Via di Stabia to be parts of a commercial artery between Naples and the Sorrento peninsula.
[60] Von Gerkan, in *Stadtplan*, p. 27, maintains that an alignment, which later disappeared, existed between the ancient east gate and the Via di Nola. Furthermore, he thought there was a market square at the site of the baths of the Forum, as at Rome.

dell'Abbondanza joins the *decumanus* of the old city and from this junction measures slightly less than twenty actus. The Via Stabiana is also twenty actus long. The plan of Pompeii is based on precise dimensional criteria.

There are three major *cardines*: the Strada di Mercurio, the Strada del Foro, the Forum itself, and the Strada delle Scuole make up the first; the second is the Strada Stabiana; the third is the street leading from the Porta Nucerina. This last is the only street at right angles to the *decumanus*, the other two being slightly oblique. The first *cardine* was laid out on an axis with the Forum, but the reasons for the shift in the Via Stabiana are not clear.

The irregular pattern of the blocks of Region VI derives from the oblique angle of the first *cardine*, while the trapezoid and parallelographic plans of the blocks adjacent to the Via Stabiana depend on the inclination of the Via Stabiana.[61]

Several other irregular features also result from the juncture of the second phase with the preexisting city, especially in areas adjacent to the original Pompeii. Vico delle Terme and Vico Storto relate to the access roads of the ancient center, as von Gerkan has observed.

The short sides of the blocks, measuring an actus or less,[62] are arranged along the *decumanus* according to the usual rule. Variations in length occur according to the location of narrow streets parallel to the *decumanus*. Thus the northern strip has two rows of blocks; those in the first row are approximately four times as long as their width, the second row is only two and one-half times the width. Two rows also make up the middle strip, with length-to-width ratios of 3:1 and 3.5:1. The blocks in the third strip have slightly less than a 2:1 ratio of length to width.

Considering that the connection of the old city to the new posed many problems, the large Pompeii is quite uniformly arranged. Curiously, this fact has not been recognized in such penetrating studies of Pompeii as those by von Gerkan,[63] who thought that only the archaic city had been planned, not the new one. In fact, almost the opposite is true. If the new city was indeed planned as a unit, one important consequence for Pompeii's history was that it did not develop gradually but grew rather as a *neapolis* im-

[61] It is for these simple reasons that the trapezoidal blocks were laid out thus, and not because of a supposed relation to the terremare (as Haverfield, *Ancient Town-Planning*, p. 67, maintains).

[62] Between 33 and 35 meters.

[63] *Stadtplan*, p. 13; *Röm. Mitt.*, 58, 1943, p. 176.

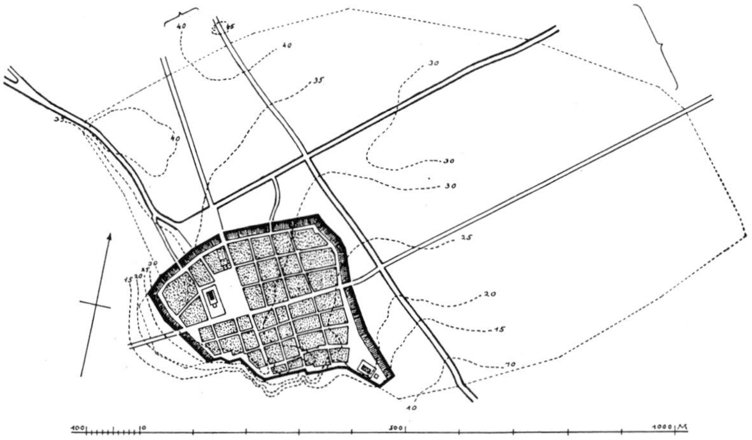

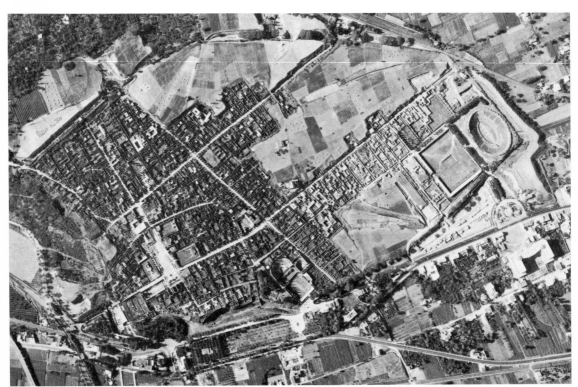

Figure 9 The original center of Pompeii and the streets extending beyond the city (von Gerkan).

Figure 10 Aerial view of Pompeii (British School of Rome). British Crown rights reserved.

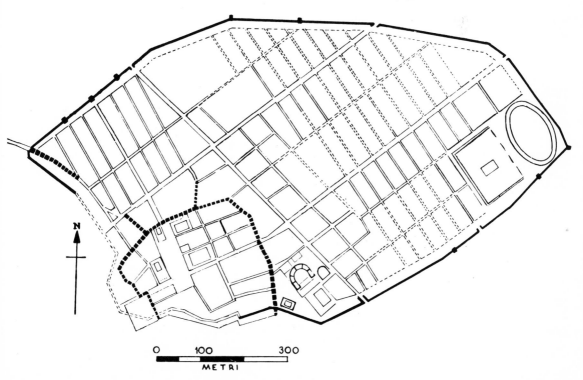

Figure 11 Plan of Pompeii. The heavy dotted lines show the original center of the city and the extra-urban streets.

N

0   100   300
METRI

29

planted *ex novo* at a definite juncture in time. Even so, it may
not have been constructed all at the same time. In this connection, it is interesting to note that in the zone adjacent to the
amphitheater there are typical blocks, laid out in the usual
pattern but not built upon, only bounded by enclosing walls.
The streets here are closed by gates fixed in pillars of tufa,
whence Maiuri[64] maintains that passage on these streets was
governed by *itinera privata* (private passages) intended exclusively
for access to the restricted areas of the gymnasium and amphitheater. Because of this use, there are neither shops nor dwellings
here. Yet, instead of limiting the function of this area to serving
the needs of the amphitheater and gymnasium, one can understand it as part of the master plan. The walls close off the building lots;[65] the roads are as yet unopened to normal traffic.[66]
Thus there was a real master plan which prescribed the development of the unbuilt city. The earlier development, too, must
have followed this system.

The city walls aid in establishing a date for the founding of the
new city (Fig. 12). Remains of walls between Porta Ercolano and
Porta Vesuvio have been put by Maiuri[67] as antedating the
Samnitic period, they have the same perimeter as the Samnitic
walls. Unlike the heavy fortifications the Samnites traditionally
built in hard and durable stone, these walls are built in local
sandstone or tufa. They mark the return of the Greek peoples
between 474 and 425 B.C. after the battle of Cumae. The chronology which Maiuri proposes finds a parallel in the political
history of the period. The Greek positions against the Etruscans
were reinforced after the battle of Cumae. Naples was also
founded at this time. Not only were the Greeks responsible for
these walls, but according to Maiuri[68] they laid out Region VI on
a "Hippodamean," not an Etruscan, plan. Indeed, since we have
shown that the new city was designed as a whole, not only was
Region VI laid out at this time but all the rest as well, following
the same plan. The new Pompeii is very probably a direct relative
of Naples; the two large new cities were developed as extensions
of the old ones after the battle of Cumae, and both were patterned by Hippodamean plans. The only difference is that at
Naples the juncture with the old city produced no complications
of boundaries.

[64] *Not. Scavi*, 1939, p. 196.
[65] An intermediate phase of development is the so-called Villa di Giulia Felice
which partially fills the block. Other blocks were provisionally used.
[66] The walls were rebuilt several times. They were laid out in very ancient days.
[67] *Mon. Lincei*, 33, 1930, p. 217; *Mem. Acc. Italia*, series 7, 4, 1944, p. 141.
[68] *Mem. Acc. Italia*, series 7, 4, 1944, p. 141.

Figure 12 A street in the eastern part of Pompeii. The walls enclose blocks that have not been built on.

The chronology advanced by von Gerkan[69] (and adopted by Boethius[70]), attributing the development of new Pompeii to the Samnitic immigration, is less likely. And nothing can be said in favor of Carrington's assignment of the new Pompeii to an Etruscan colony of about 500 B.C.[71] He finds in the plan a resemblance to the Italic urban schemes, and the trapezoidal blocks are suggestive of the terremare.[72]

Concluding our remarks on greater Pompeii, we can say that by attributing to the Greeks the unified plan of Pompeii, not only do we clarify the general framework of the Etruscan and Greek influences upon planning but we also flatly eliminate the theory that Region VI was built by Etruscans.

As for archaic Pompeii, its nucleus may date from the sixth century. It has nothing in common with the Greek system of several *decumani*; it is simply an axial scheme, even though the *decumanus* is not perfectly rectilinear. Pompeii belongs to a general category of ordered cities and, as described by von Gerkan, can be defined as a "pure Italic example,"[73] without limiting that type of urban pattern to the Italic peoples, however. There are no particular reasons to consider Pompeii an Etruscan city, as Spano would,[74] nor to justify Etruscan influence upon the city by the existence of three gates (according to van Gerkan[75]) and a temple with three *cellae* (though this has a later date). Most probably the plan layout dates from before the period of Etruscan influence in Pompeii and was built instead by the Oscans and the Greeks of the Gulf of Naples (compare the Temple of Apollo to the Doric temple).[76]

Πλατεῖαι and στενωποί

The conventional terms *decumanus* and *cardine* have been employed for the streets of Pompeii, meaning respectively the longitudinal and transverse streets. Instead, πλατεῖαι and στενωποί ought to be used for the major communications arteries (Via dell'Abbondanza, Via Stabiana, and others) and for the secondary streets. Many of these στενωποί secondary streets, whose function is less that of channeling traffic than of defining the city blocks, are bounded by long walls with no doors and few windows, because

[69] Including the completion of the master plan as well as the chronology of the walls.
[70] A. Boethius, "Gli Etruschi in Pompei," in *Symbolae Danielsson*, Uppsala, 1932, p. 1.
[71] R. C. Carrington, "The Etruscan and Pompeii," in *Antiquity*, 6, 1932, p. 5.
[72] See footnote 61.
[73] *Röm. Mitt.*, 1943, p. 173.
[74] *La Campania Felice*, p. 180.
[75] *Stadtplan*, p. 16.
[76] See especially Maiuri, *Mem. Acc. Italia*, series 7, 4, 1944, p. 122 ff., 146.

whenever possible the preferred access was onto the πλατεῖαι.
These same terms could be used just as well for what excavators
have called the "avenues" and "streets" of Olynthus. The terms
are documented in the description of two comparable cities,
Thurii and Naples—the latter for the πλατεῖαι. It would be
highly anachronistic to search for *cardines* and *decumani*; in fact
the widespread disparity in ascribing the status of *cardine* or
decumanus to one street or another is significant. Spano's explanation of the "dekkviarim" (*decurialis*) inscribed in the Stabian gate
(Conway 39) as "decumanus" cannot be supported.[77] (This is
the name he gave to the Via dell'Abbondanza.) The etymological
significance of the terms πλατεῖα and στενωπός is usually preserved;[78] I cannot agree with Dalman's opinion that, as used in
the new comedy, they have lost their original meaning.[79] Dalman
notes that a scene of *Adelphoe* by Hegesippos takes place in a
στενωπός. This must refer to a main street because people pass
through (παριὼν πᾶς) and because the door of a house opens onto
it. He therefore argues that it must have been a πλατεῖα instead,
and that στενωπός must have been used in this sense. However,
house doors and the passage of people are also possible on the
"streets" of Olynthus and through the lanes and alleys of Pompeii.
Up to now these have been called στενωποί, even by Lucian
(*Dial. Mer.* 9, 5, where a farcical duel takes place in a στενωπός
and *ibid.* 2, 3, an allusion to a door decorated with a crown).[80]

The Latin *platea* and *angiportus* correspond to the Greek terms
πλατεῖα and στενωπός, as already noted by Nissen.[81] Their
equivalence is especially clear in the work of Vitruvius, as will
be shown, and in the glossarists. The etymology of *angiportus* is
close to στενωπός (*angu* meaning "narrow" and *portus* "passage").[82]
Its principal meaning is therefore that of a "narrow passage"
(that is, a communicating street), while the meaning of "blind
street" remains secondary.[83] Varro can be cited in this connection too; he writes in *De ling. Lat.* VI, 41: *qua nihil potest agi*

[77] G. Spano, "Porte e regioni pompeiane," in *Rend. Acc. Napoli*, 17, 1937,
p. 323. See also G. O. Onorato, *La sistemazione stradale del quartiere del Foro
triangolare di Pompei*, in *Rend. Lincei*, series 8, 6, 1951, p. 250.
[78] Pollux IX, 37: τὰς δὲ στενὰς (ὁδοὺς) στενωπούς καὶ λαύρας. The generic explanation by Hesychius is not valid: Στενωπός· ἡ ἀγυιά καὶ πλατεῖα καὶ ἄμφοδος. The
obvious meaning of alleys is found in the passage of Aristides quoted on p. 17.
[79] C. O. Dalman, "De aedibus scaenicis comoediae novae," in *Klass. Phil.
Studien*, 3, Leipzig, 1929.
[80] Likewise the στενωπός στενός of Nicostratus (24 K) is not decisive,
as Dalman (*De aedibus* p. 69) would believe it to be.
[81] H. Nissen, *Pompeianische Studien*, Leipzig, 1877, p. 541.
[82] See Paul. Fest. 16 L. See also J. André, *Les noms latins du chemin et de la rue*, in
Revue Et. Lat., 1950, p. 124.
[83] *Schol. Hor. Carm.* I, 25, 10: *angiportum alii dicunt vicum sine exitu* (others call
the angiportum a way with no exit). Cf. also *Gloss.* II, p. XII.

(some of the alleyways of Pompeii were closed to traffic).

Angiportus, as translated from the στενωπός of Greek comedy, has lost its original etymological meaning, according to Harsch,[84] and has come to mean only *street*. His demonstration of this is analogous to what was said by Dalman. In Plautus's *Pseud.* 960–961; Terentius's *Eun.* 845, the *angiportus* cannot be "blind street" but rather a place where there are people, an ordinary street onto which face many houses. It follows that the term no longer has a specific meaning, and the *angiportus* were not blind streets onto which no house had its principal entry. Unfortunately the conclusions regarding the meaning of στενωπός and *angiportus* in the comedy were based precisely on this mistaken supposition.

At Pompeii, a city divided by πλατεῖα and στενωπός, we can easily picture scenes from the Latin and new Greek plays. The two terms, for street and lane, alternate in the plays, but it should be noted that *platea* occurs frequently in Terence and Plautus but is rare elsewhere; it was probably borrowed from Greek comedy. The lanes are given ordinal numbers: a τρίτη ῥύμη ("sixth street"; ῥύμη is equivalent to στενωπός) is mentioned in Philippides 22 K, and Plautus speaks of an *angiportus*, *sextum a porta proximum*, which means the sixth in a series of lanes opening onto a main street beginning at a gate.[85] Whenever possible, people sought to have the main entrance to their house face the *platea*, with a rear gate from the garden opening onto the *angiportus* (Plautus *Asin.* 741; *Most.* 1045). Such is the layout of the houses of the Tragic Poet, of Pansa, and others. A similar situation is recorded in Apuleius *Met.* IX, 2, in which a bitch enters the house *de proximo angiportu per posticam*.[86]

Of particular importance are the passages from Vitruvius referred to in Chapter 2, footnote 11 and the one cited here, from I, 7, 1: *Divisis angiportis et plateis constitutis arearum electio . . . est explicanda. . . .* (After apportioning the alleys and settling the main streets, the choice of the squares has to be explained.) It follows that the urban structure consists of *plateae* and *angiportus*, that is, πλατεῖαι and στενωποί. The latter certainly are not blind alleys, but rather narrow lanes or streets (as they are used in contrast to *plateae*) and are fundamental to the urban pattern. Their relationship

---

[84] P. W. Harsch, "Angiportum, platea and vicus," in *Class. Phil.* 32, 1937, p. 34. Instead, in Terence, *Adelphus*, p. 574, a distinction is made between *plateae* and *angiporti*.

[85] See also Apuleius, *Met.* III, 2.

[86] Harsch, p. 48, n. 9, notes that *platea* and *angiportus* are not used interchangeably in Apuleius *Met.* II, 32 and III, 2 as Jordan claims (*Topographie der Stadt Rom*, I, 1, p. 523, n. 49a).

and orientation have always been the object of close study. It would seem that Vitruvius considers Greek cities, rather than Roman ones, to be patterned by πλατεῖαι and στενωποί. In the example cited by Vitruvius, the urban structure is set by a grid of *angiportus* and *plateae*; the piazzas can be placed only secondarily within this grid. This is exactly what is done in the uniformly patterned Greek and Roman cities.

Not unlike the preceding examples, Herculaneum is laid out along *decumani* parallel to the sea (one 7 m, the other about 5 m wide). These are crossed by narrower *cardines*. The blocks, however, are not of the usual dimensions. As far as we know from the excavations to date, they are some 47 meters wide to either 90 (a ratio of 1 to 2) or 120 or more meters long.

Herculaneum

Theophrastus had written of Herculaneum as early as 314 B.C.[87] No other documents of its origin are available.[88]

The plan layout of Naples (Fig. 13) in the modern part of the city has been closely studied by Beloch,[89] and the reconstruction of the original plan has closely followed the guidelines he set up.[90] The high city is patterned by four (three according to Beloch) *decumani*, which are *a, b, c,* and *d* in the plan (Fig. 14),[91] and 20 *cardines* (22 or 23 according to Beloch). The *decumani* run some 25 degrees north of east–west, paralleling the coast line.

Naples

From this pattern emerge elongated rectangular blocks which according to De Petra[92] have the following dimensions: the *decumani* are 20 feet (6 m) wide; the blocks measure 185 meters on the long side (a measure apparently based on 1 stadium); the residential city in the direction of the *cardines* measures 740 meters (4 stadia); the short side of each block, including the *cardine*, averages 37 meters; the *cardines* vary in width from 10 to 12 feet (2.96 to 3.55 m). According to De Petra, the 37-meter width of the blocks represents 125 Euboic feet (0.296 m per Euboic foot). It is more probable that the blocks are one actus wide. In any case, the ratio of width to length is about 1:5. The

[87] Theophrastus, *Hist. Plant.* IX, 16, 6.
[88] According to Spano ("Porte e regioni," p. 215) the plan is Etruscan.
[89] J. Beloch, *Campanien*, 2nd ed., Breslau, 1890, p. 66. Also in *Bull. Inst.* 1877, p. 9.
[90] B. Capasso (and G. De Petra) *Napoli greco-romana*, Naples, 1905; A. Pirro, *Le origini di Napoli* II, Salerno, 1906; E. Gabrici, "Contributo archeologico alla topografia di Napoli," in *Mon. Lincei* 41, 1951, p. 552, especially p. 652.
[91] These are respectively: Vicolo S. Marcello; Via S. Biagio–Via Vicara Vecchia; Via dei Tribunali; Via Pisanelli–Anticaglie–SS. Apostoli.
[92] See Capasso, *Napoli*, p. 103, 135.

Figure 14 Diagrammatic reconstruction of the old city of Naples.

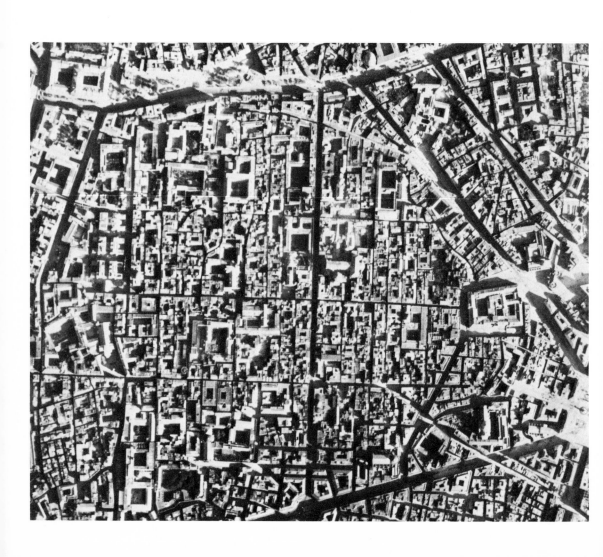

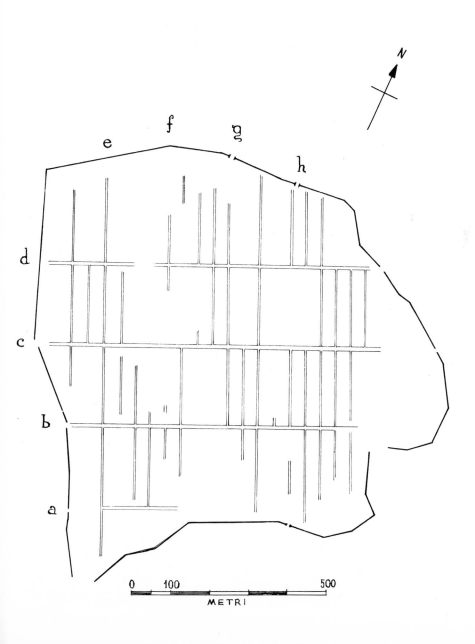

N

e   f   g

h

d

c

b

a

0   100   500
METRI

blocks, with the *cardines* between them also measure 740 meters, again using De Petra's calculations.

On the other hand, Pirro claims that not all the *cardines* are equal but that four are wider than the others.[93] He reaches this hypothesis in his desire to reconstruct Naples along the pattern of Thurii;[94] however, the method he employs in the analysis of the major streets is arbitrary.

Actually, the medieval topology of the city is a good guide to a study of the ancient streets.[95] While the greater number of streets were called *vici*, some were said to be *plateae*. These latter (see Fig. 14) correspond to *decumanus b* (Platea Nili–Platea Furcillensis), *c* (Platea Ficariola–vel ad duos amantes–Platea Augustalis–Platea Capuana), *d* (Platea Marmorata–Summa Platea), and to the *cardines e* (Platea Atriensis) and *f* (Platea subtus forum). Furthermore, the location of certain medieval gates is known. Those which correspond to the four *decumani* seem to be certain.[96] In addition, there was a gate near the back door of San Gennaro (near *g*) and two others, it appears, opened in the north and south walls on the axis of Via Donnaregina (*h*).[97] These last two gates might lead one to postulate the existence of two other πλατεῖαι *g* and *h*,[98] in which case the north–south πλατεῖαι, would have been spaced at regular intervals of four actus. Although the reconstruction of these elements remain in doubt, the distinction between πλατεῖαι and στενωποί is documented by the medieval tradition of *plateae* and *vici*. As at Thurii, Naples was structured by a basic pattern of a few mutually perpendicular πλατεῖαι and the insertion among them of στενωποί.

The date of the founding of Naples remains uncertain. According to Beloch,[99] the city was at first an Athenian colony. He bases his view on texts by Strabo (page 246) and others which show Athenian influence, borne out also by characteristics of the coinage.[100] If this view is correct, Naples was founded after

[93] Those corresponding to present-day streets: Zite–S. Agostino; Duomo; S. Gregorio Armeno; S. Gaudioso–Nilo.
[94] He furthermore believes that the plan is inscribed in a circle, thus the κύκλος τετράγωνος of Aristophanes (cf. p. 67).
[95] Cf. B. Capasso, *Monumenta ad Neapolitani ducatus historiam pertinentia* I–III, Naples 1871–92; an excellent plan of medieval Naples is in Table XXII. There is a convenient topographic index.
[96] The topography of Porta Ventosa (near *a*) is not clear.
[97] See Capasso, *Napoli*, p. 146.
[98] The corresponding names are: *e*) Via Atri–Nilo–Università; *f*) a section of via S. Paolo; *g*) Vicolo S. Petrillo–Gerolomini; *h*) Via Donnaregina–Zuruli. A *platea Nustriana* is also known (perhaps it corresponds to the Via S. Gregorio Armeno), as is a *platea S. Ianuari*.
[99] *Companien*, p. 30.
[100] Timeus, in *Schol. ad Lycophr.* 732; Tuc. VI, 81, 3.

446 B.C., remarkably close to the date of the founding of Thurii (444–443), as Nissen too has stated.[101]

However, the coinage that began at about 460 B.C. leads to a different conclusion.[102] As a result, it is usually believed that Naples was founded after the return of the hegemony of Syracuse, after the battle of Cumae in 474. At that time Partenope (Palaepolis) gained new vigor through rapid urban expansion, so important as to merit the name of Neapolis.[103] It is to this city that the necropolis with ceramics of the third decade of the fifth century is attributed.[104] And it is very probable that it was this installation of a "new city" that brought about the general and unified master plan that has been discussed, and not the date of the walls, as established by Gabrici[105] on the basis of the ceramics gathered in the first excavation. (The ceramics are thought to date from the first half of the fourth century.) Although it is believed that the walls belong to the period of Samnite rule, they may have been built as additional fortifications later in the life of the city.[106]

Pozzuoli and Sorrento

Pozzuoli and Sorrento are considered in the same general framework as Naples, and are usually ascribed to the Greek period (sixth or fifth century B.C.). However, because they differ from the previous examples and because no single archeological element could confirm the traditional chronology, it is probable that they belong to a later era.

Paestum

The aerial photographs of Paestum reproduced in Figs. 15 and 17 were taken by Lieutenant Colonel G. Schmiedt on August 4, 1954. He was quick to observe that the clearly visible strips in the

[101] *Italische Landeskunde* II, p. 747. It is compared to Thurii because of its Hippodamean plan.
[102] A. Sambon, *Monnaies antiques de l'Italie*, I, Paris, 1903, p. 171; L. Breglia, in *Parola del Passato* 7, 1952, p. 286.
[103] Concerning this chronology and the often questioned relationships between Palaeopolis and Naples, see G. Pugliese–Carratelli, *Parola del Passato* 7, 1952, p. 243; M. Napoli, *Realtà storica di Partenope, ibid.* p. 269; see also Berard, *La Colonisation Grecque de l'Italie et de la Sicilie*, Paris 1941, p. 71. It is possible that contrary to what the reference in the obscure passage of Livy (VIII, 22) would have one believe, Naples and Paleopolis were not two distinct cities. In Dionysius of Halicarnassus's narrative (XV, 5) of the same events he does not speak of Paleopolis, while instead the Fasti trifonali (326) register the triumph *de Samnitibus Palaeopolitaneis.*
[104] Gabrici, "Contributo archeologico," p. 650, 671.
[105] *Ibid.*, p. 663.
[106] Concerning the line of the city walls, see also M. Napoli, *Parola del Passato* 7, 1952, p. 442. I am indebted to the kindness of Dr. Johannowsky for the information that as a result of recent research the walls of Naples are known to have been built in successive phases, the earliest of which dates from the middle of the fifth century B.C.

Figure 15 Aerial view of Paestum
(Istituto Geografico Mil.).

Figure 16 Reconstruction of
Paestum.

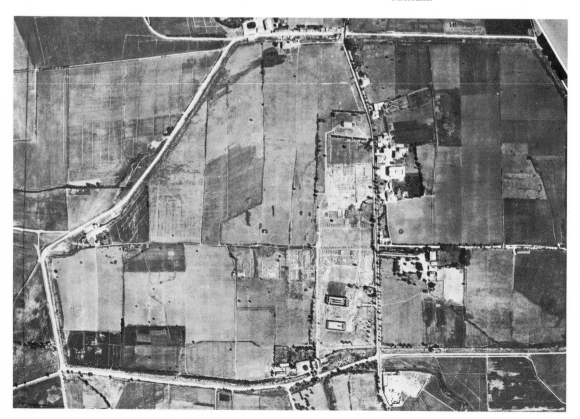

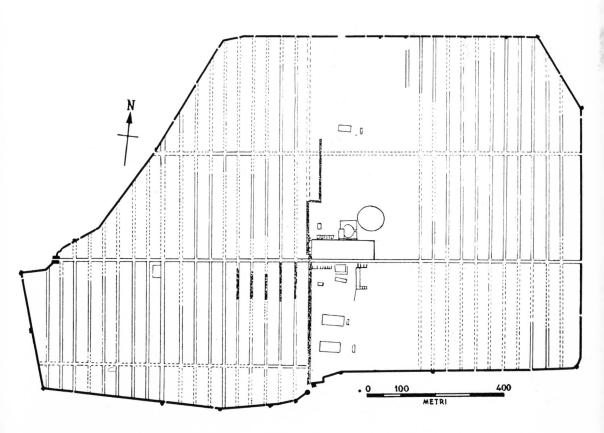

N

● 0   100   400
        METRI

area reveal some of the ancient road patterns (Fig. 16).[107]
Through other photographs J. Bradford[108] confirms this observa-
tion, as do aerial surveys by the Istituto Geografico Militare,
undertaken before the excavations by Sestieri.

Reconstructed through information gained by excavations and
aerial photographs, the plan of Paestum is of extraordinary
interest. A *decumanus* crosses the city from east to west (from
Porta Sirena to Porta Marina), cutting the Forum along its
southern edge. The remains of a parallel road to the south can
be traced through the aerial photograph. This road must have
extended only into the western sector of the city, for in the eastern
part it is replaced by the line of the walls.

Furthermore, the part of the city to the north of the principal
decumanus is twice the width of the southern sector.[109] Hence,
another *decumanus* to the north of the main one probably divided
the city into three equally spaced strips. Short traces of such a
road can be seen in the photographs. Yet aligned with this
postulated third *decumanus* are two *posterulae*, small gates, built
into the walls. The gate on the eastern side is unusual in width
and shape; furthermore, it should be noted that there are very
few gates on this side. Each of the three bands thus defined is
about 300 meters (1000 feet) wide.

A few *cardines* have been found through excavations. The one
behind the sanctuaries in the southern sector, leading from the
Porta della Giustizia to the Forum (the so-called Via Sacra),
has no clear continuation into the northern sector. To the west
of the Forum there are several lanes. No street appears to correspond to the Porta Aurea. Four *cardines* to the west of the Via
Sacra have been excavated, though for only a short tract. Each
is between approximately 4.90 and 5.40 meters in width. Many
other *cardines* can be discerned in the photographs. The towers
in the walls are often seen to be aligned with these, and the same
is true of the frequent *posterulae*. (This explains why there are so
few *posterulae* on the east side.)

A grid of very long rectangles results, the short sides of which
measure about 35 meters (34.55 m at the last excavated block
to the west) by 300 meters, a ratio of 1:8.5. As at Pompeii,

[107] G. Schmiedt, F. Castagnoli, *L'Universo* 35, 1955, no. 1, p. 10.
[108] Paper delivered at the II Congress of Classical Studies, Copenhagen,
August, 1954.
[109] Considering the line of the walls and, to the west, the partial remains of
the *decumanus* mentioned earlier.

42

Figure 17 Aerial view of the central part of Paestum. (Istituto Geografico Mil.).

whose blocks measuring 230 meters in length were subdivided into two or three sections, the long blocks of Paestum must have been traversed by small lanes. This system must also have been employed at Naples. It is entirely probable that not all the *cardines* were as narrow as those excavated to the west of the Via Sacra. Perhaps some were much wider, truly major communication arteries comparable with the *decumani*,[110] while the others were simple access ways to residential blocks. This arrangement would have formed a system of πλατεῖαι and στενωποί, as at Pompeii.

Although the sanctuaries are oriented directly east, the city grid is shifted a few degrees north of east.[111] Possibly religious considerations dictated that the temples should be positioned more carefully by celestial orientation without regard to the layout of the city. Yet it can also be hypothesized that the master plan of the city evolved after the sanctuaries had been built, since the relation between the two plans is not always coherent. Several early constructions belonging to the sanctuary (to the south of the Forum) are buried under buildings that follow the general grid pattern of the city.

According to this hypothesis, the present urban structure is not the original one but is later than the "basilica" and the "Temple of Ceres," although not necessarily later than other sanctuaries near the basilica, including the Temple of Neptune. (These presumably were aligned with the basilica to create a general uniformity.) Thus the layout of Paestum should be dated no earlier than the end of the sixth century.

On the other hand, we know that the city grid was laid out before the end of the fifth century. The most ancient walls are placed at about 400 B.C. by Krischen[112] and, as we have seen, the large gates, small gateways, and towers are aligned with the city grid. Not much later than the period of the walls are several buildings near the Forum which are aligned with the city grid, including perhaps the cistern and especially a large building east of the road which joins the eastern part of the Forum with the region of the two southern sanctuaries.[113]

We should also remember that during the fifth century Paestum

---

[110] The ninth *cardine* (from porta Marina) seems to fit this description.
[111] Von Gerkan (*Griechische Städteanlagen*, Fig. 7), though doubtful, considers the city to be oriented toward the north.
[112] F. Krischen, *Die Stadtmauern von Pompeji . . .* , Berlin, 1941, p. 23.
[113] C. P. Sestieri, *Paestum*, Rome, 1953, p. 23, dates these at the fifth century B.C. The chapel recently discovered between the temple of Ceres and the Forum has an orientation between that of the city and that of the sanctuaries.

must have had a large expansion, as indicated by the vast quantity of archeological material from this era. Such an expansion has been interpreted by P. Zancani-Montuoro[114] as related to colonization by Sybarites. This hypothesis derives from the new interpretation by C. P. Sestieri[115] and P. Zancani-Montuoro, working independently, of a passage by Strabo (V, 251) relative to Posidonia: Συβαρῖται μὲν οὖν ἐπὶ θαλάττῃ τεῖχος ἔθεντο, οἱ δ' οἰκισθέντες ἀνωτέρω μετέστησαν, ὕστερον δὲ Λευκανοὶ μὲν ἐκείνους, Ῥωμαῖοι δὲ Λευκανοὺς ἀφείλοντο τὴν πόλιν. (The Sybarites, it is true, had erected fortifications on the sea, but the settlers removed them farther inland; later on, however, the Leucani took the city away from the Sybarites, and the Romans in turn took it away from the Leucani.) The two authors claim that the τεῖχος near the sea must be the walls of Posidonia and not other primitive fortifications, as previously thought.[116] They thereby distinguish a Sybarite colony from the first settlements of the οἰκισθέντες, who then migrated toward the interior. (These people are thought to be Thessalians by Zancani-Montuoro and Enotri by Sestieri.) The colonization by Sybarites must have happened at the end of the seventh century according to Sestieri. The colony is also recalled by Pseudo–Scimmo. Yet Zancani-Montuoro claims that the colony could only have been founded after the destruction of the mother country in 510 B.C. It could have been founded immediately afterward, as the present author thinks, or during the long rebuilding of the city state. A city called Sybaris also existed from 510 to 453 B.C.[117] Again, Zancani-Montuoro[118] recalls that the coinage of the sixth century seems to proclaim the independence of Posidonia from Sybaris and that certain coins dating certainly after 480 commemorate both cities and can therefore be placed at the time of the participation of Posidonia in the rebuilding of Sybaris, 453–448.[119] Breglia[120] accepts the evidence of the coins but thinks that in the years following 510 B.C. a large number of Sybarites arrived at Posidonia, causing a great expansion.[121] An incuse coin (therefore earlier

[114] P. Zancani–Montuoro, "Sibari, Poseidonia e lo Heraion," *Arch. Stor. per la Calabria e la Lucania* 19, 1950, p. 65.
[115] C. P. Sestieri, "Le origini di Poseidonia," *Archeol. Class.* 2, 1950, p. 180; "Ancora sulle origini di Poseidonia," *ibid.* 4, 1952, p. 77; "Ricerche posidoniati," *Mel. Ec. Franç.* 67, 1955, p. 35.
[116] As Maiuri would believe ("Origine e decadenza di Paestum," *Parola del Passato* 6, 1951, p. 274). See also M. Guarducci, *Arch. Class.* 4, 1952, p. 149, n. 4.
[117] See Dunbabin, *The Western Greeks*, Oxford 1948, p. 365.
[118] "Sibari," p. 81.
[119] Head, *Historia nummorum*, p. 84; Dunbabin, loc. cit.
[120] L. Breglia, "Le monete delle quattro Sibari," *Annali Ist. Ital. Numismatica* 2, 1955, p. 9.
[121] Remembering that the population of Sybaris, including farmland, was placed at half a million (Dunbabin, op. cit.).

than 480), and with the stamp of Sybaris, is attributed to Posidonia because it is a part of the local measuring system. However, this is a unique piece.

Leaving aside the possibilities of linking the development of Paestum's master plan to the Sybarite colony and waiting for thorough excavations to ascertain certain elements, one must perforce include in the chronology of the city plan a very long blank period, the whole course of the fifth century, with the walls as an *ante quem* reference.

Capua

The regular pattern of ancient Capua has already been surveyed by Beloch.[122] He recognized in the present plan of Santa Maria Capua Vetere a division by *cardines* and *decumani* (among the latter the Corso Umberto, corresponding to the Via Appia). The plan devised by Heurgon (Fig. 18)[123] traces five *decumani*, designating the central one as the major axis, and four *cardines*.

Capua occupies a prominent place in the study of uniform town planning because it is considered one of the rare examples of the Etruscan plan.[124] It has the intersection of two main axes, *decumanus* and *cardine*, that typify the Etruscan type and differentiate it from the nearby Greek cities patterned by rectangular blocks. Indeed, the importance of the comparison is heightened by the proximity of Capua to the Greek cities and the possible relations between them. Did the Etruscans of Capua imitate the neighboring Greek cities, as Thulin thinks? Or should Capua be considered a pure example of Etruscan planning and the bridge by which the Greeks learned the grid layout? (Lehmann-Hartleben).

But the reconstructions that have been made of a city divided by *cardines* and *decumani* are unsatisfactory. The *decumanus* that corresponds to the extension of the Via Appia (Corso Umberto) is not perfectly rectilinear. More important, the *cardines*, as reconstructed by Heurgon, are not parallel to each other. As yet there is nothing to compare with the exceptional width of the blocks (150 and 200 m by 200 and 300 m). Excavations so far have not provided sufficient evidence upon which to make an accurate reconstruction. However, important results are expected from the research of A. De Franciscis. The reconstruction proposed here is only speculative.

[122] *Campanien*, p. 344.
[123] J. Heurgon, "Capoue préromaine," *Bibl. Ec. Franç.* 154, 1942, p. 118.
[124] P. Ducati, "La città etrusca," *Historia* V, 1931, p. 8; also Heurgon, "Capoue," p. 121.

The aerial photograph (Fig. 19) presents a section of the outlying territory as well. The *cardines* and *decumani* of the centuriation do not reach into Capua; they bear no relation to the pattern of streets in the city.[125] The boundaries between city and territory are thus clearly marked. By extending the line of the Via Appia to the east and west we can link two gates not far from the bends in the road.

These findings agree with the few and insufficiently documented archeological data—the location of the tombs immediately outside the city, the remains of the gates near the San Prisco bridge,[126] and some foundations of walls between San Francesco and the Amphitheater.

Compared to the reconstructions of Capua by Beloch and Heurgon, the configuration of the perimeter walls is probably less regular. One element of the centuriation lines indicates that the eastern wall must run closer to the city center.[127] The city would thus have had a north–south extension of 40 actus and an east–west run of 46 actus (Fig. 20).

The *decumanus* commonly assigned to the path of Corso Umberto may be in a different position. The city was probably patterned by six equally spaced *decumani*, five of which correspond to existing streets. It remains uncertain whether the second of these from the north is Corso Umberto or if it follows the path as laid out in the reconstruction (which would correspond better to the change of direction of the Via Appia on the west and would be more regular on the eastern side). The first, third, and fourth strips (from the south) measure one stadium each, as at Naples; the others are a little larger.

Via R. D'Angiò, apparently related to the Via Dianae, is an irregular *cardine* of which a fragment has recently been found.[128] Perhaps the path of the other two *cardines* is ancient, though they too are irregular, especially to the east (Corso Garibaldi, Via Albana).

[125] My statements to the contrary in *Bull. Com.* 72, 1946–48, p. 51, are incorrect. I judged that according to the topographic maps the Corso Umberto was an extension of a road in the centuriated territory (this was the so-called *decumanus*, according to Beloch).

[126] *Campanien*, p. 346, 357, 345.

[127] A median element of the centuriation near Piazza Girolamo della Valle. The section of road recently found to the west of S. Erasmo was probably part of a road that ran along the outside of the walls (see A. De Franciscis, *Not. Scavi* 1952, p. 316).

[128] Near the corner with via Torre (*ibid.*, p. 269).

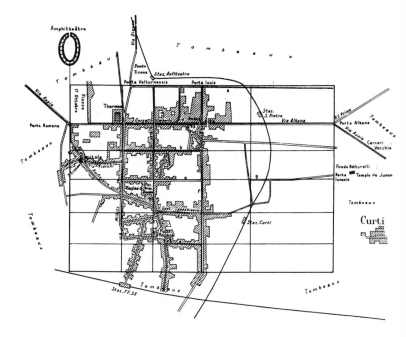

Figure 18 Capua as reconstructed according to J. Heurgon.

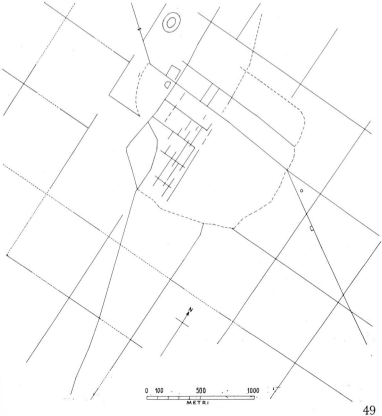

Figure 19 Aerial photograph of Capua (British School of Rome). British Crown rights reserved.

Figure 20 Capua as diagrammatically reconstructed.

0   100   500   1000
METRI

49

Between the *decumani* the aerial photographs show clear elements of a design of *strigae*, one actus wide, to be seen in the pattern of narrow lanes or in the disposition of the buildings.[129] This follows the common scheme of *decumani* subdivided into sections of uniform width, *strigae*. The major *cardines* do not follow such a rigorously perpendicular layout. Yet it would be foolish to attribute the irregularities to medieval or modern changes, since the streets are fully consistent with the patterns of external circulation and since the truer directions are closely maintained through the *decumani* and minor *cardines*. There is no need to correct the major *cardines*, then, as in the reconstructions; they probably represent preexisting roads.

A regular pattern is observable in only one part of the city. The southwest sector follows a different layout that can be explained either as a medieval modification of the city or, more probably, as the oldest residential sector, already in existence before the master plan was devised. The fact that this section was joined to important extraurban roads argues in favor of this latter hypothesis. Furthermore, it may be readily supposed that Capua, a city of vast dimensions, must have been preceded by a more modest center. Its history would thus be analogous to that of Pompeii.

No archaeological traces are to be found today in the eastern half of the city, because the decline of Capua caused the number of residential neighborhoods to decrease. It is likely that, as at Pompeii, this outermost sector of the city was the last to be built and was later abandoned when the medieval settlements gravitated toward the center.

This is the general character of Capua, which can be deduced with a fair degree of probability. A reference to the city plan comes to us from Cicero, *De leg. agr.* II, 35, 96: *Romam in montibus positam et convallibus, cenaculis sublatam atque suspensam, non optumis viis, angustissimis semitis, prae sua Capua planissimo in loco explicata ac prae illis spatiis irredebunt atque contemnent.* . . . (Rome, situated on mountains and in valleys, raised and suspended in the air with its houses, its poor streets and narrow alleys, they derided and contemned in comparison with their Capua developed on a plain, and in comparison with those spaces.) *Spatiis* is a correction made by Haupt. The codes give *semitis*, and Clark gives *praeclarissime*.

---

[129] Such as the Via Riccio and Vico Casertano.

The plan corresponds in full to the traditional Greek scheme. As Beloch has observed, the Via Appia, which presupposes the city, is an *ante quem* reference to the city (312 B.C.). Yet Velleius, I, 7, makes two very different references concerning the founding of Capua: *nam quidam . . . aiunt a Tuscis Capuam Nolamque conditam ante annos fere DCCCXXX . . . sed M. Cato quantum differt, qui dicat Capuam ab eisdem Tuscis conditam ac subinde Nolam; stetisse autem Capuam, antequam a Romanis caperetur, annis circiter CCLX.* (For some maintain that . . . eight hundred and thirty years ago, Capua and Nola were founded by the Etruscans . . . but the opinion of Marcus Cato is vastly different. He admits that Capua, and afterwards Nola, was founded by the Etruscans, but maintains that Capua had been in existence for only about two hundred and sixty years before its capture by the Romans.) That is, 800 and 470 B.C.;[130] yet both dates are incorrect, by general agreement. As was pointed out before, the plan of a city as large as Capua probably does not go back directly to the original founding but grew alongside a more ancient nucleus. This we recognize as the western part, to develop at a later time into a great *neapolis*. Various sources suggest that it had the nature of a double city.[131] The date ascribed by Cato to the city can be understood as a reference to the *neapolis*.

Yet if, as seems probable, we see in Capua an Etruscan plan, we cannot fail to observe how similar the plan is to those of neighboring Greek cities. The city does not offer an Etruscan system (as in the preceding reconstructions which established a *decumanus maximus*) to contrast with that of the Greek cities.

At the opposite end of the Etruscan world is Marzabotto (Fig. 21), which has been considered a clear example of a city laid out according to the Etruscan discipline.[132] The theories of division by perpendicular axes, *decumani* and *cardines*, known through literary sources, are supposedly confirmed through this monumental example. Furthermore, age and geographic location have invited comparisons between Marzabotto and villanovan Bologna, and especially between Marzabotto and the terremare

Marzabotto

[130] In fact as De Sanctis notes (*Storia dei Romani* I, p. 445, no. 1), we must disagree with Beloch that Cato attributes the capture of Capua to 338 or 343. See also Heurgon, *Capoue* p. 63.
[131] Heurgon, *Capoue*, p. 122.
[132] See especially E. Brizio "Relazione sugli scavi eseguiti a Marzabotto presso Bologna," in *Mon. Lincei* I, 1889, c. 249; A. Grenier, *Bologne villanovienne et etrusque*, Paris, 1912, p. 32; G. Patroni, *St. Etr.* 7, 1933, p. 56; P. E. Arias, "Considerazioni sulla città etrusca a Pian di Misano (Marzabotto)," in *Atti e Mem. Deput. St. Patria Prov. Romagna* N.S. III, 1953, and by the same author in *Mostra dell'arte e della civiltà etrusca*, Milano, 1955, p. 148; J. B. Ward Perkins, *Town Planning Review* 26, 1955, p. 132.

Figure 21 Marzabotto (Brizio).

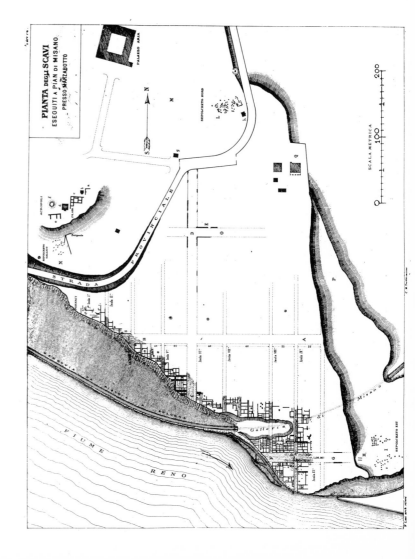

settlements. The plan of villanovan Bologna had already been thought of as orderly and uniform. Further comparisons with the terremare settlements have made Marzabotto an important element in developing the theory of Etruscan origins.

The founding of the city is generally placed toward the end of the sixth century or the beginning of the fifth century B.C. Notwithstanding the width and the high quality of workmanship of the streets and the relative perfection of the sewer system, the city cannot be dated later than the middle of the fourth century B.C., when the Gallic invasion brought destruction.

The plan is identical to that of Naples; two *decumani* (east–west) crossed by a perpendicular street. The rectangular blocks, usually one actus wide, are established on the *decumani*. (As at Olynthus, a block twice the normal width is divided by an *ambitus*.) The blocks are about 165 meters wide,[133] slightly less than those at Naples. As at Piraeus, the *decumani* are 15 meters wide.

A detailed comparison with the layouts of Naples, Paestum, and Olynthus shows that Marzabotto does not depend at all on the Etruscan theory of delimitation, nor can it be compared with the terremare cities; it is essentially a Greek city. The types of residential units have been rightly compared by Arias with those at Olynthus. There is no usual Etruscan axial system but instead πλατεῖαι and στενωποί which delineate the *strigae* of the city blocks.

It is truly remarkable that Lehmann–Hartleben[134] should find in Marzabotto an extraordinary resemblance to the terremare plans and nothing whatever in common with Greece. On the other hand, Brizio and especially Patroni and Sogliano have compared Marzabotto with the urban structure of Pompeii, but from this they deduced that Pompeii was Etruscan in origin.

This chapter has documented a characteristic subdivision *per strigas* through various examples dating between the end of the sixth and into the fifth century B.C. Not always has it been possible to establish a firm date. Having examined individual cities, we will now try to look at them as a group.

The date proper for Miletus, whose plan differs slightly from the general scheme, is about 479 or 466 B.C. Olynthus and Rhodes are datable at 432 and 408, respectively. Agrigento was probably

---

[133] Two series of blocks are 10 actus long.
[134] *Realencyclopaedie* IIIA, c. 2033.

built in 480 or 450. Naples belongs to the third decade of the
fifth century, while Pompeii is assigned to between 474 and 425.
Paestum can be traced from between the end of the sixth century
and the beginning of the fourth. The date of Capua is difficult
to establish. Marzabotto could go back to the first decades of the
fifth century, and certainly not later than the first half of the
fourth.

Although some dates are uncertain and perhaps too elastic, there
is a certain contemporaneity among the sites.

Furthermore, evidence indicates that the Etruscan cities of Capua
and Marzabotto are planned according to Greek schemes.
Obviously an interdependence must exist between plans having
specific characteristics in common (even in the measuring system
employed); in other words, there is imitation by either Etruscans
or Greeks of the other. It is possible to advance the view, as
Lehmann–Hartleben has done for the origins of uniform town
planning, that the idea was Etruscan and that the Greeks came
to know the system at Capua, subsequently propagating it
through Sicily and the entire Greek world.

Yet general historical reasons prevail, such as the superior civilization of the Greeks, and in particular their interest in mathematics and meteorology from the sixth century on. The Greeks
were also colonizers, to a much greater extent than the Etruscans,
and this meant a greater concern for planning in connection
with the founding of cities. All these considerations argue in
favor of Greek priority.

Capua, after the building of a first nucleus, was enlarged with the
aid of a master plan copied from various Greek cities. Marzabotto
naturally was in contact with the Greek world through the port
of Spina. The plan of Marzabotto must be attributed to the Greek
influence which so deeply penetrated the Etruscans of the north
during the fifth century, and especially during the middle
decades.[135]

From this survey there also arises greater appreciation of the
community of civilization which ties the Etruscans to the Greeks.
Not only were the Etruscan artistic forms derivative (easily
obtainable through commercial exchange) but they also copied
the city plans with absolute fidelity.

[135] Cf. G. Vallet, "Athènes et l'Adriatique," in *Mel. Ec. Franç.* 42, 1950, p. 33;
P. E. Arias, "Testa arcaica di Marzabotto," in *Riv. Ist. Naz. Arch. St. Arte,*
N.S. I, 1952, p. 242.

Chapter 2

The Greek City

The preceding chapter did not deal with the simple orthogonal
layout of buildings and roads but with two important systems,
that of the intersections of major axes and that of the highly
disciplined and rigorous grid plan which almost invariably
follows the *per strigas* layout.

The latter pattern is of special interest. Throughout the search
for the "Hippodamean" cities in early ages and in the Minoan–
Mycenaean culture as well as in the East, no distinction was
made between the simple rectangular layout and the grid pattern.
Undoubtedly, the rectangular layout is a common basis for
organization found in Egypt, Mesopotamia, and in Minoan
palaces. At Thermi IV,[1] at Troy (even though there is a circular
wall), and at Phylakopi there is rectangular order within the
uniform subdivisions. This is also true at Palaikastro, Gurnia,[2]
Vroulia,[3] and Naucratis.[4] This rectangular plan, which continues
through the fourth-century Greek world and into the Hellenistic
age and which was adopted also by the Romans, is not defined
only by the principal of orthogonality; it also has the following
characteristics:

1. A master plan provides for development of the total area
within the walls as well as that of the residential sector. The few
major arteries are made to run longitudinally. There is no
central intersection. There are some perpendicular axes and many
streets parallel to them, subdividing the city into elongated
blocks, usually one actus wide. The grid of subdivisions is the
same throughout the city. Squares and public buildings are
inserted into the grid without destroying the subdivision, since
they are treated as part of the blocks. In this case the streets are
tangential to the buildings and squares. Obviously all of this
represents a well thought-out system.

2. The preeminent concern of the urbanist is revealed in his study
of residential quarters, which are subdivided by uniform equal
blocks and whose houses are alike in style. All houses face the
street.

These characteristics and the master plan to control future expansion are reflected in a passage from Plato (*Leg.* VI, 779B)

[1] There are here three parallel roads: W. Lamb. *Excavations at Thermi in Lesbos*,
Cambridge, 1936.
[2] See an important survey by R. W. Hutchinson. "Prehistoric Town Planning
In and Around the Aegean," in *Town Planning Review* 23, 1952–53, p. 261;
24, 1953–54, p. 5.
[3] K. F. Kinch, *Vroulia*, Berlin, 1914.
[4] H. Prinze, "Funde aus Naukratis," in *Klio*, vol. 7, 1908, p. 11, Table 1.

which states that the houses are to be alike and even proposes, for that purpose, that all the foundations be laid at the time the city is founded:

ἀλλ' εἰ δὴ τεῖχος γέ τι χρεὼν ἀνθρώποις εἶναι, τὰς οἰκοδομίας χρὴ τὰς τῶν ἰδίων οἰκήσεων οὕτως ἐξ ἀρχῆς βάλλεσθαι, ὅπως ἂν ᾖ πᾶσα ἡ πόλις ἓν τεῖχος, ὁμαλότητί τε καὶ ὁμοιότησιν εἰς τὰς ὁδοὺς πασῶν τῶν οἰκήσεων ἐχουσῶν εὐέρκειαν, ἰδεῖν τε οὐκ ἀηδὲς μιᾶς οἰκίας σχῆμα ἐχούσης αὐτῆς, εἴς τε τὴν τῆς φυλακῆς ῥᾳστώνην ὅλῳ καὶ παντὶ πρὸς σωτηρίαν γίγνοιτ' ἂν διάφορος.[5]

It is difficult at present to document this type of city planning before the beginning of the fifth century B.C. If we can confirm some innovations as having occurred in that century, we remove the difficulty commonly associated with the dating of the Hippodamean plan, which is that Hippodamean cities have existed since the beginning of the seventh century. In any case, greater knowledge should be gained concerning this style of planning and how it began. Quite possibly Eastern cities were known and used as examples: for instance, the village of Kahun (Fig. 22), built for the workers of the pyramid of Sesostris II (1897–1879 B.C.),[6] and also some parts of Tell-el-Amarna (Fig. 23), rebuilt *ex novo* in 1396–1354 B.C.[7] Accounts by Herodotus reveal that during the fifth century there was widespread interest in the Orient.

It is possible that these urban forms derive entirely from rational criteria of organization, not necessarily inspired by earlier examples. For instance, the Aztec city of Tenochtitlan (Fig. 24)[8] exhibits not only the rectangular layout (at least in some parts) and the astronomical orientation but also an analogous scheme of an east–west *decumanus* and many north–south *cardines*, setting off elongated *strigae*.

Such a design could correspond to precise, basic criteria. For instance, the reasoning could be that only a few roads are needed for circulation, while the rest serve to subdivide the city into sections. The blocks become long and narrow because houses are small, and thus a series of houses can form a *striga* without the

[5] "But if men really must have a wall, then the building of the private houses must be arranged from the start in such a way that the whole city may form a single wall; all the houses must have good walls, be built regularly and in a similar style, facing the roads, so that the whole city will have the form of a single house, which will render its appearance not unpleasing, besides being far and away the best plan for ensuring safety and ease for defense."
[6] W. M. Petrie, *Illahun, Kahun and Gurob*, London, 1891, Table XV.
[7] *The City of Akhenaten* I (E. Peet and C. L. Wooley), 1923, p. 51, Table XVI; III (J. D. S. Pendlebury), 1951, pp. 122, 189. Compare H. W. Fairman, "Town Planning in Pharaonic Egypt," in *Town Planning Review* 20, 1949, p. 33; J. Vandier, *Manuel d'archéologie égyptienne* II, Paris, 1955, p. 972.
[8] See F. Violich, *Cities of Latin America*, New York 1944, figures after p. 28.

Figure 22 Kahun (Petrie).

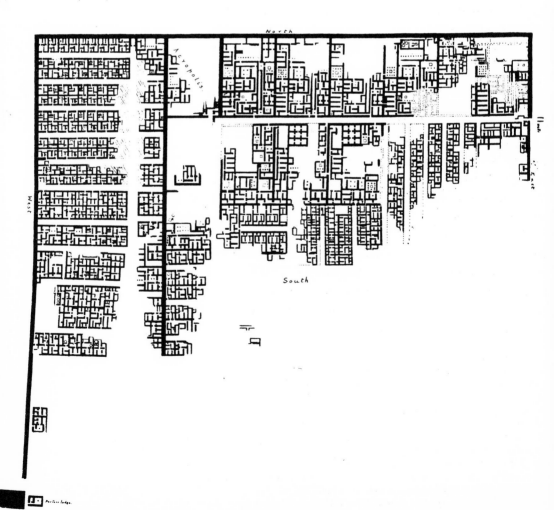

Figure 23 Tell-el-Amarna
(*The City of Akhenaten*).

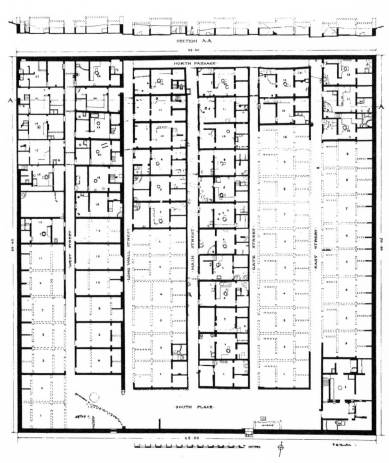

59

Figure 24 Tenochtitlan (Violich).

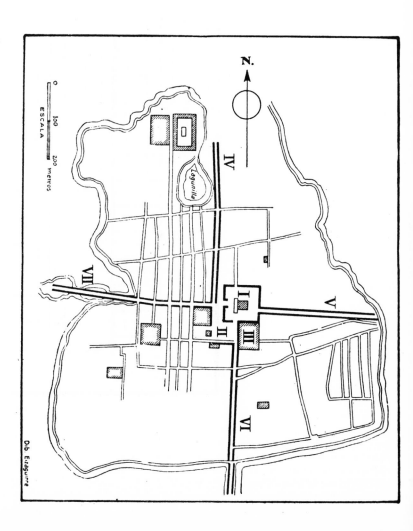

need of superfluous *decumani*. Protection from wind and sun is
an obvious reason for adopting an astronomical orientation in the
plan.[9]

Orientation

Decumani usually run east–west, or nearly so (Posidonia, Capua,
Marzabotto, Agrigento, and later Priene, Damascus, Laodicea;
Pompeii is almost northeast), north–south (Rhodes, Olynthus),
or parallel to the coast line (Naples, Herculaneum, and Alexandria). Von Gerkan[10] rightly excludes the religious significance
in orientation, and instead points to hygienic and topographic
criteria. Though perhaps inspired by Hippocrates (*de aere, aquis,
locis*), Aristotle (*Pol.* VII, 10, 11, 1330a) testifies to the care
taken to open the city to winds (preferably the east, otherwise
the north). Oribasius[11] prefers an east–west, north–south array
of streets. On the other hand, Vitruvius[12] counsels against

---

[9] It is not employed in coastal cities.

[10] *Griechische Städteanlagen*, p. 78. This is also valid for the most ancient cities.
Because the north–south orientation of squares and courtyards (and thus of the
entire urban complex), as at Gurnià, Phestos, and Tyrins is employed for
practical criteria such as the right exposure to the sun, we must not look for
sacred symbolism of the celestial orientation in the Hymn to Apollo 55: Φοίβῳ
δ᾽ ἑσπόμενοι πόλιας διεμετρήσαντο / ἄνθρωποι· Φοῖβος γὰρ ἀεὶ πολίεσσι φιληδεῖ /
κτίζομένης᾽, αὐτὸς δὲ θεμείλια Φοῖβος ὑφαίνει. (And Phoebus it is that men
follow when they map out cities. For Phoebus evermore delights in the founding of cities, and Phoebus himself doth weave their foundations.) See Fabricius,
in Pauly-Wissowa, *Realencyclopaedie* IIIA, c. 2000.

[11] II, p. 318 (Bussemaker–Daremberg): Ἐν πόλει, ὅταν ἀγυιαὶ παράλληλοι
ὑπάρχωσιν, ἀεὶ μὲν καὶ εἰς μῆκος ἀλλήλαις, καὶ ἀεὶ δὲ εἰς πλάτος ,ταῖς ὁμοταγέσι μὲν
ἀνατολῇ ἰσημερινῇ καὶ δύσει ἐπὶ εὐθείας κείμεναι, αἱ δὲ ἄρκτῳ καὶ μεσημβρίᾳ, πᾶσαι
δὲ τέμνωσι τὴν πόλιν, αἱ μὲν κατὰ τὸ μῆκος ὅλον, αἱ δὲ κατὰ τὸ πλάτος μέχρι περάτων, οὐδὲν
οἰκοδόμημα τὸ μεταξὺ ἑαυτῆς ἑκάστη ἔχουσά τι ἐνιστάμενον, ἐπὶ πολὺ τῶν προαστείων
καθαρὰς ἐπὶ εὐθείας τὰς ἐπὶ ἑαυτῇ ἑκάστη ἔχουσα ὁδοὺς, εὐάερον τὴν πόλιν παρέχουσιν,
εὐήλιόν τε καὶ καθαρὸν καὶ εὐήνεμον τὸ κατάστημα ποιοῦσιν, ὅτι οἱ ἄνεμοι, βορέας καὶ
νότος, εὖρος τε καὶ ζέφυρος ... διαρρέουσι ... Εὐήλιόν τε τὴν πόλιν οὕτως ἔχουσαι ποιοῦσιν
αἱ ἀγυιαί, ὅτι ἥλιος ἀνατέλλων καὶ δυόμενος εἰσέρχεται, τὰς κατ᾽ ἀνατολὴν ἐπὶ εὐθείας,
μεσουρανῶν δὲ εἰς πάσας τὰς κατ᾽ ἄρκτους καὶ μεσημβρίας, ὥστε ἡλιοῦσθαι ἑκάστης ἡμέρας
ἐν τῇ πόλει τὰς ἀγυιάς. (If all the streets in a city are parallel, some lengthwise and
others widthwise; and if streets in the same direction face either the rising and
setting sun or the north and south; if they all intersect the city to its farthest limits,
either by length or by width; if none of them contains in its whole length any
building that may prove to be an obstacle; if the suburban streets that are a
continuation of these carry on the same line and are unobstructed for a great
distance—then these streets will ventilate the city well, will expose it to the
winds, and light it by the sun. And the city will be clean, because the winds,
that is the winds of the north, south, east, and west, which are the most important of all and the most ordered, will traverse the streets easily, since the
streets lie in the same directions. And since the winds will meet no obstacle
to their passage, they will cause no violence as they blow across the city; for
indeed the winds when they meet no impediment pass without one's knowing.
Nevertheless, they do not traverse the whole city without influence, for they
purify the environs, ridding the city of smoke, dust, and all kinds of exhalations.
Streets thus disposed render the city easy of access to the sun, because it penetrates the city at its rising and at its setting. At its rising it enters on a straight
line into the streets that are turned to the east; at noon it penetrates those
that are facing the north or the south. Thus all the streets of the city are subjected daily to the influence of the sun. . . .)

[12] Vitruvius I, 6, 1: *Moenibus circumdatis sequuntur intra murum arearum divisiones*

opening the streets to winds. The orientation of the streets was also concerned with the correct exposure of the house to sunlight. Xenophon[13] and Aristotle[14] favor a southern exposure. To the north of each courtyard there was a covered porch called a *pastas*,[15] protected from the north winds and open to the sun. This kind of porch is frequently seen in Olynthus.[16]

Residential Sectors

The system just described follows from still other considerations. A scheme permitting a unifying equality within the residential sectors, without a focus to the plan, is certainly adapted to a democratic society based on equality among its citizens. Aristotle (*Pol.* VII, 1300b, 17 ff) explains the relation between city planning and politics by affirming that an acropolis is proper to an oligarchy and a monarchy, while the flat areas are part of a democracy. It is worthy of note that this type of urban design developed in the fifth century, after the fall of tyranny and the affirmation of democratic constitutions. The criteria of equality

---

platearumque et angiportûm ad caeli regionem directiones. Dirigentur haec autem recte, si exclusi erunt ex angiportis venti prudenter. Qui si frigidi sunt, laedunt; si calidi, vitiant; si umidi, nocent. . . . *cum septentrio* . . . *in angiportis et plateis non possunt consistere propter vehementiam frigoris.*
(When the walls are set round the city, there follow the divisions of the sites within the walls, and the layings out of the broad streets and the alleys with a view to aspect. These will be rightly laid out if the winds are carefully shut out from the alleys. For if the winds are cold they are unpleasant; if hot, they infect; if moist, they are injurious. [Vitruvius then cites the case of Mytilene where] . . . when the north wind blows . . . nobody can stand in the alleys and the streets for the cold.)
I, 6, 7: *Tum per angulos inter duas ventorum regiones et platearum et angiportorum videntur deberi dirigi descriptiones.* (Then the angles between two quarters of the winds will determine the laying out both of the streets and of the alleys.)
I, 6, 13: . . . *inter angulos octagoni gnomon ponatur, et ita dirigantur angiportorum divisiones.* (. . . let the gnomon be set upon the angles of the octagon and let the division of the alleys be directed accordingly.)
[13] *Mem.* III, 8, 9: Οὐκοῦν εἴ γε καλῶς ἔχει ταῦτα οὕτω γίγνεσθαι, οἰκοδομεῖν δεῖ ὑψηλότερα μὲν τὰ πρὸς μεσημβρίαν, ἵνα ὁ χειμερινὸς ἥλιος μὴ ἀποκλείηται, χθαμαλώτερα δὲ τὰ πρὸς ἄρκτον, ἵνα οἱ ψυχροὶ μὴ ἐμπίπτωσιν ἄνεμοι . . . (If, then, this is the best arrangement, we should build the south side loftier to get the winter sun and the north side lower to keep out the cold winds.)
Oecon. IX, 4: Καὶ σύμπασαν δὲ τὴν οἰκίαν ἐπέδειξα αὐτῇ ὅτι πρὸς μεσημβρίαν ἀναπέπταται, ὥστε εὔδηλον εἶναι, ὅτι χειμῶνος μὲν εὐήλιός ἐστι, τοῦ δὲ θέρους εὔσκιος. (I showed her that the whole house fronts south, so that it was obvious that it is sunny in winter and shady in summer.)
[14] *Oecon.* I, VI, 7–8 (1345a): Καὶ πρὸς εὐημερίαν δὲ καὶ πρὸς ὑγίειαν δεῖ εἶναι (οἰκίαν) εὔπνουν μὲν τοῦ θέρους, εὐήλιον δὲ τοῦ χειμῶνος. Εἴν δ᾽ ἂν ἡ τοιαύτη κατάβορρος οὖσα καὶ μὴ ἰσοπλατής. (For well-being and health, again, the homestead should be airy in summer, and sunny in winter. A homestead possessing these qualities would be longer than it is deep; and its main front would face the south.)
[15] Vitruvius, VI, 7, 1: *Id peristylum in tribus partibus habet porticus inque parte, quae spectat ad meridiem, duas antas inter se spatio amplo distantes, in quibus trabes invehuntur* . . . *Hic locus apud nonnullos prostas, apud alios pastas nominatur.* (This peristyle has porticoes on three sides, and on the side that looks south has two doorposts rather distant one from the other, on which are placed the architraves . . . This place by some is called *prostas*, by others *pastas*.)
[16] *Excavations at Olynthus* 8, p. 143, 161.

naturally were felt much more in the colonies. The relation
between colonies and uniform city planning has been frequently
dealt with, beginning with Nissen. However, Nissen is interested
in the problem only from the seventh century on.

It would prove of great interest to study the house plan and its
siting on the one-actus-wide block, particularly in relation to the
standardized urban blocks. At Olynthus the block is bisected
on its short side by an *ambitus*; the long side of 86.34 meters is
divided into five parts. Thus, each house occupies a square,
one-half actus on a side. An analogous relationship between
block and house has been found by Arias[17] to exist at Marzabotto. The dimensions of the house at Soluntum are similar.

The blocks containing the oldest houses in Region VI at Pompeii
are also divided into two parts on their short side, near the
decumanus (Casa del Naviglio and Casa del Fauno on the Via di
Nola, and Casa del Labirinto on the Via di Mercurio). More
frequently the entire width of the blocks is occupied between one
cardine and another, although in some cases this may have resulted
from the expansion of single houses. There is no evidence for
Ippel's rigidly schematic reconstruction of the plan.[18] The relation
of the house to the astronomic orientation of the city has already
been discussed.

From the viewpoint of urban aesthetics such a rigid geometric
plan may seem surprising among the Greeks; it would find
greater credence among the Romans. Yet such a system is a
Greek creation; it was not only practical but fashionable in its
time. Heraclitus I, 1 (third century B.C.)[19] judges the plan of
Athens κακῶς ἐρρυμοτομημένη διὰ τὴν ἀρχαιότητα (streets irregularly
divided because of their antiquity). He is critical of the houses,
affirming that a stranger would hardly believe this to be the
famous city of Athens and to be reassured would need to see the
theater, the Parthenon, or the Olympieion—in other words,
monuments rather than urban forms. These and other judgments
on the older forms as well as the new planning are very significant.

Yet this Greek creation (not Hellenistic, since it appears as early
as the fifth century) is not really alien to the Greek spirit, which
sought through mathematics the precision of temple architecture
and in some cases of sculpture as well.

---

[17]See Chapter 1, note 132, p. 51.
[18]A. Ippel, "Pertica Pompeiorum," *Röm. Mitt.* 46, 1931, p. 198. Bisecting the
block was also common at Herculaneum, although the short side of the block
was not the same width as at Pompeii.
[19]*Sitzb. Akad. Wiss. Wien* 227, 2, 1951, p. 72.

The rigor of geometric subdivision was maintained even in difficult geographic situations, on steep slopes, as for example in Rhodes and Olynthus first, then in Soluntum and Priene, among others. Interesting scenic effects were often obtained this way.

Master Planning

Finally, the importance of the concept of a master plan cannot be ignored. It anticipated the future growth of the city to prevent building outside the walls and imposed a design to be followed through gradual growth and construction. Bearing in mind this use of the plan, we must concede that it is not a trustworthy criterion of urban texture and population even though it has always been used as such. (Beloch[20] uses the physical extension of the city to calculate its population.)

As we have seen, Hellenistic city planning focused on private construction. Yet the agora, too, took on the general character of the plan and fitted into the grid, as evidenced by its perpendicular sides. A homogeneous architecture arose from its regularity of plan, evidenced especially in a single style of arcades. Pausanias apparently refers to this type of agora when he contrasts the ancient agora at Elis, built on the old plan, to that of Ionian cities: VI, 24, 2: Ἡ δὲ ἀγορὰ τοῖς Ἠλείοις οὐ κατὰ τὰς Ἰώνων καὶ ὅσαι πρὸς Ἰωνία πόλεις εἰσὶν Ἑλλήνων τρόπῳ δὲ πεποίηται τῷ ἀρχαιοτέρῳ στοαῖς τε ἀπὸ ἀλλήλων διεστώσαις καὶ ἀγυιαῖς δι' αὐτῶν. (The agora of Elis is not after the fashion of the cities of Ionia and of the Greek cities near Ionia; it is built in the older manner, with porticoes separated from each other and with streets running through them.)[21]

[20] J. Beloch, *Die Bevölkerung der griechisch-römischen Welt*, Leipzig 1886, p. 474.
[21] See F. Tritsch, "Die Agora von Elis und die altgriechische Agora," *Oest. Jahresh.* 27, 1931–1932, p. 64; R. E. Wycherley, "The Ionian Agora," *Journ. Hell. Stud.* 62, 1942, p. 21; R. Martin, "Recherches sur l'agora grecque," *Bibl. Ec. Franç.* 164, 1951, p. 372.

Chapter 3

Hippodamus
of Miletus

Aristotle (*Pol.* II, 1267b, 21) tells that Hippodamus of Miletus[1] studied the theory of government and advised segregation of the people by class; furthermore τὴν τῶν πόλεων διαίρεσιν εὗρε, although some scholars do not attribute this passage to Aristotle. Elsewhere Aristotle goes on to speak of the uniform patterning of streets (*Pol.* VII, 1330b, 21): ἡ δὲ τῶν ἰδίων οἰκήσεων διάθησις ἡδίων μὲν νομίζεται καὶ χρησιμωτέρα πρὸς τὰς ἄλλας πράξεις, ἂν εὔτομος ᾖ καὶ κατὰ τὸν νεώτερον καὶ [2] τὸν Ἱπποδάμειον τρόπον, πρὸς δὲ τὰς πολεμικὰς ἀσφαλείας τοὐναντίον ὡσ εἶχον κατὰ τὸν ἀρχαῖον χρόνον· δυσέξοδος γὰρ ἐκείνη τοῖς ξενικοῖς καὶ δυσεξερεύνητος τοῖς ἐπιτιθεμένοις. (The arrangement of the private dwellings is thought to be more agreeable and more convenient for general purposes if they are laid out in straight streets, after the modern fashion, that is, the one introduced by Hippodamus; but it is more suitable for security in war if it is on the contrary plan, as cities used to be in ancient times; for that arrangement is difficult for foreign troops to enter and to find their way about in when attacking.)

Moreover, Hippodamus is called architect by Harpocration and by Photios, μετεωρολόγος by Hesychius and Photios.

The lines of Aristotle reveal only a concept of the ordered city. It should be possible to glean more knowledge through the study of those cities assigned to Hippodamus,[3] such as the rebuilt Piraeus ("during the Persian wars," *Schol. ad Arist. Eq.* 327), the original layout of Thurii (444–443 B.C.) and Rhodes (408–407 B.C.), but these are spread over too wide a period of time. Moreover, the evidence for the plan of Rhodes is not altogether authentic, and the founding of Piraeus probably goes back to the time of Pericles. The date appears to be confused with that for the city walls.[4] In any case, Piraeus and Thurii are generally recognized as the work of Hippodamus; von Gerkan, who establishes his birth at about 500 B.C., believes that he may have also worked on the reconstruction of Miletus.

Piraeus, in fact, was Hippodamus's most famous work: τὸν Πειραιᾶ κατέτεμεν (Aristotle II, 1267b, 22), and a square was named Ἱπποδάμειος ἀγορὰ (Xenophon *Hell.* II, 4, 11). One can

---

[1] Concerning Hippodamus, see M. Erdmann, *Hippodamos von Milet und die symmetrische Städtebaukunst der Griechen, Philologus* 42, 1884, p. 193; E. Fabricius in Pauly-Wissowa, *Realencyclopaedie* VIII, 2, c. 1731, IIIA, c. 1992; A. von Gerkan, *Griechische Städteanlagen*, p. 42; G. Cultrera, "Architettura ippodamea," *Mem. Linc.* 5, 17, 1923, p. 361; I. D. Kondis, Ἡ εὔτομος διάθεσις εἰς τὸν Ἱπποδάμειον τρόπον, Ἀρχ. Ἐφημ. 1953–1954, p. 255.

[2] According to some authorities, καὶ is to be omitted or to have only an explicative function.

[3] Information gathered in particular from Erdmann's article.

[4] Judeich, *Topographie von Athen*. p. 76, n. 2.

also refer to *Schol ad Arist. Eq.* 327 and the passages of several lexicographers—Harpocration, Hesychius, Photios, and others—which assign only Piraeus to Hippodamus. The city almost certainly was patterned on an orthogonal grid, with a principal street some fourteen to fifteen meters wide.

The urban pattern of Thurii is also attributed to Hippodamus. He is known to have been a citizen of the colony and to have participated actively in its inception (Hesychius). The plan was laid out on an orthogonal grid, and it may even have been subdivided *per strigas*.

The layout of Rhodes must not be overlooked, either. Even though it is incorrectly attributed by Strabo to Hippodamus (XIV, 654: ἡ δὲ νῦν πόλις ἐκτίσθη κατὰ τὰ Πελοποννησιακὰ ὑπὸ τοῦ αὐτοῦ ἀρχιτέκτονος, ὥσ' φασιν, ὑφ' οὗ καὶ ὁ Πειραιεύς—the present city was founded at the time of the Peloponnesian war by the same architect, as they say, who founded the Piraeus), still it has characteristics that are not unlike the Hippodamean plan, and indeed the attribution to Hippodamus no doubt arose through its similarity. As reconstructed by Kondis, the plan layout of Rhodes (page 16) follows an orthogonal pattern, and in some parts it is clearly subdivided *per strigas*. It certainly did not have a radial scheme as some writers have thought, who picture it as a city laid out on the pattern of Karlsruhe and Palmanova.[5]

More generally, since Aristotle distinguishes the old irregular city from the new Hippodamean type, we should mention that the system generally in use in Aristotle's time was basically orthogonal.[6]

A passage from Aristophanes' *The Birds* (995–1009 B.C.) is frequently interpreted as a reference to Hippodamus:

Αριστοφανης and the Circular City

Με. γεωμετρῆσαι βούλομαι τὸν ἀέρα ὑμῖν διελεῖν τε κατὰ γύας. Πει. πρὸς τῶν θεῶν σὺ δ' εἶ τίς ἀνδρῶν; Με. ὅστις εἴμ' ἐγώ; Μέτων, ὃν οἶδεν Ἑλλὰς χὠ Κολωνός. Πει. εἰπέ μοι, ταυτὶ δὲ σοι τί ἔστι; Με. κανόνες ἀέρος. αὐτίκα γὰρ ἀήρ ἐστι τὴν ἰδέαν ὅλος κατὰ πνιγέα μάλιστα. Προσθεὶς οὖν ἐγὼ τὸν κανόν' ἄνωθεν τουτονὶ τὸν καμπύλον ἐνθεὶς διαβήτην—μανθάνεις;

---

[5] See, for example, Haverfield, *Ancient Town-Planning*, p. 14.
[6] Although the new system may not be identifiable with the Hippodamean system (see ref. 2 above), the latter may be a particular element within the new planning system. Although highly praised by Aristotle, the plan is criticized for its lack of security when compared with the old irregular city which was difficult to assail. Thus he advises that the regular subdivision be limited to certain areas of the city and that a layout by συστάδες τῶν ἀμπέλων be adopted, which according to Kondis are terraces (see the reference to Kondis's article, ref. 1).

Πει. οὐ μανθάνω. Με. ὀρθῷ μετρήσω κανόνι προστιθείς, ἵνα ὁ κύκλος
γένηταί σοι τετράγωνος κἂν μέσῳ ἀγορά, φέρουσαι δ᾽ ὦσιν εἰς αὐτὴν ὁδοὶ
ὀρθαὶ πρὸς αὐτὸ τὸ μέσον, ὥσπερ δ᾽ ἀστέρος αὐτοῦ κυκλοτεροῦς ὄντος
ὀρθαὶ πανταχῇ ἀκτῖνες ἀπολάμπωσιν. Πει. ἄνθρωπος Θαλῆς. (Metone: "I
wish to survey the air and divide it into plots" [or "into roads"].
Peistheitairos: "By the gods, what kind of man are you?" M.:
"Who am I? Metone, known in Hellas and Colonos!" P.:
"Say, what stuff is this?" M.: "These are measures for air. You
must know that the air, taken in its entirety, more or less re-
sembles an oven. Thus, I, applying to it from above this curved
edge, and inserting a compass . . . understand?" P.: "No, I do
not understand." M.: "With the straight rule which I shall
apply, I will measure so that the circle is squared. In the center
there will be a square and in it will converge all the straight
roads, such as in a star, itself also round, the rays emanate to all
directions." P.: "This man is a Thales!")

Possibly τετράγωνος is not just "square" or "four-cornered" as is
often thought, because the squaring of the circle, so expressed,
is not really humorous. Probably the first meaning (according to
Erdmann) is taken to be "quadripartite," and thus the squaring
of the circle, understood in a double sense, becomes wittier.
Thus we have essentially a circular city divided by two orthogonal
axes that meet at the agora in the center. There follows the
comparison to the rays of a star which spread from the center in
every direction. If this comparison is taken literally, the vision
of a "Place de l'Étoile" arises. But such a plan was not employed
until the seventeenth century; it was totally unknown to the
ancient world. Though it is true that the poet can create before
the architect,[7] a less literal interpretation of the passage would
be appropriate: the rays are the four streets which, spreading
from the agora, define the quadripartite city.[8]

It is unclear, however, whether the passage should be interpreted
as paradoxical and fantastic or, as seems more probable, as a
simply comic reference to contemporary planning practices and
theories. If there is an allusion in the passage, is it to Hippodamus? Hermann and Erdmann think so, and talk of Hippodamus's cyclic principle, which they relate to the school of
Protagoras. This brings to mind radial and semicircular plans,

---

[7] A. Kriesis, *Urbanism in Greece* (given at the Congress of Classical Studies,
Copenhagen, 1954), p. 23, believes that Aristophanes had anticipated such
a town-planning scheme by many centuries.
[8] Which was a complete set of radial roads, according to R. E. Wycherley,
"Aristophanes, The Birds 995–1009," in *Class. Quart.* 31, 1937, p. 22.

as seen by Cultrera, Friedländer, and others. Von Gerkan rules out all of this.

The evidence of Piraeus, Thurii, and Rhodes also rule out this extension of Hippodamus's work. We have seen that the θεατρο-ειδής of Rhodes and other cities is not a reference to the form of the city. Most probably Aristophanes's allusion is to be considered as kin to Plato's fantasy of the city of Atlantis,[9] said to be laid out in concentric rings. If both Plato and Aristophanes were referring to a circular city, one wonders whether there might have been a theoretical interest in such a city,[10] a not improbable hypothesis in the light of some Oriental examples and considering the interest there might well have been in Oriental city plans, as evidenced in Herodotus. Certainly the Egyptian contribution to the myth of Atlantis is not to be overlooked.[11]

The circular city[12] was known in the Orient, as evidenced by the hieroglyphic symbol of a city—a circle divided into four parts (Fig. 25). Other examples are the Hittite city of Zincirli,[13] the Assyrian military encampments shown on reliefs (Fig. 26),[14] and the city of Qala i Darad, while Baghdad (a circular plan, from its descriptions) continues the tradition which, by other routes, extends to the Viking castles.[15] Especially important are the circular walls of Ekbatana (Herodotus I, 98).

The interest which Plato showed in the Orient is apparent to L'Orange. That Aristophanes should have shared this interest is not inconceivable. His "quadripartite" circle can certainly be

[9] Cf. P. Friedländer, *Platon*, I[2], Berlin, 1954, p. 303 ff. It is not certain whether the city mentioned in *Leg.* p. 778C is circular.
[10] R. E. Wycherley, in "Aristophanes," *Class. Quart.* 31, 1937, p. 30, thinks that the ancient circular city with a central agora was abstracted into a uniformly patterned system; yet this is not known through any of the urban examples we have studied. Perhaps it is preferable to admit a certain amount of theoretical speculation. Furthermore, we are not to confuse with this type of plan the πόλις τροχοειδής plan, the name given by Herodotus VII, 140 to Athens. These terms simply refer to a city arrayed around an acropolis, in the words of Strabo (IX, 396) ἐν πεδίῳ περιοικουμένη κύκλῳ (in a plain and surrounded by dwellings).
[11] See especially M. Pallottino, *Archeol. Class.* 4, 1952, p. 237.
[12] Which after all is also the form which many prehistoric centers approximate, also in Greece (Dimini).
[13] R. Naumann, *Architektur Kleinasiens*, Tübingen, 1955, p. 215; p. 207, Fig. 246; p. 216, n. 6, on circular fortifications found in the territory between the Tigris and Euphrates, of uncertain date.
[14] I. Billerbeck-Delitzsch, "Die Palasttore Salmanasser von Balawat," *Beiträge zur Assyriologie und semit. Sprachwiss.* 6, 1909, Table C.
[15] See the interesting study by H. P. L'Orange, "The Illustrious Ancestry of the Newly Excavated Viking Castles Trelleborg and Aggerborg," *Studies Robinson*, I, St. Louis 1951, p. 509. For a discussion of Oriental cities, see also Lavedan, p. 56, and H. W. Fairman, "Town Planning in Pharaonic Egypt," *Town Planning Review* 20, 1949, p. 33.

Figure 25 Hieroglyphic symbol of the city.

Figure 26 Assyrian military camp (Billerbeck–Delitzsch).

an allusion to theoretical discussions concerning the circular oriental city divided into four parts by axes intersecting at the center. Even though the common form of Oriental cities does not follow this plan, it is possible to understand the theoretical importance which it must have had among the Orientals: the city portrayed the world scheme, circular and quadripartite.

To summarize: The orthogonal grid layout is characteristic of the plan invented by Hippodamus. However, many cities which followed this scheme were laid out prior to his time, and it is not uncommon to speak of "Hippodamean" cities that antedate Hippodamus. According to Nissen and von Gerkan, this type of plan gained widespread use during the diffusion of the colonies in the seventh and sixth centuries B.C. Hippodamus then might be considered a symbol[16] or at best an urbanist who based his fame on theorizing a preexisting system.[17] Or, as Cultrera[18] and Pace[19] point out, the character of Hippodamean urbanism is not so much in the plan layout (which could be either orthogonal or circular[20]) as in the monumental squares, the over-all harmony, and especially the search for scenographic effects. Speaking with caution, because the evidence is certainly incomplete, we could say that Hippodamus—who perhaps was born at the beginning of the fifth century and perhaps worked on the plan for Miletus, but who certainly was an established urban designer by the middle of the fifth century—should not be associated with the simple orthogonal system of ancient origins but with that which had developed into the uniform and regular grid pattern known to exist in the fifth century.

It is also natural that such urban design did not spring full-blown from his mind. There must have been precedents from earlier decades, and Hippodamus's fame must have grown from his theoretical approach to the work. But while it is easily conceivable that he should have developed in depth these concepts of a city plan that was already being elaborated in his own time and that he should have given his name to it, it is difficult to think that his fame should be based upon a form of urbanism already two centuries old. More likely he was neither a symbol nor a simple theorizer but an urbanist who played an important

---

[16] Lavedan, *L'urbanisme*, p. 123; R. E. Wycherley, *How the Greeks Built Cities*, Macmillan, 1949, p. 16; R. Martin, "Recherches sur l'agora grecque," *Bibl. Ec. Franç.* 174, Paris 1951, p. 347.
[17] *Griechische Städteanlagen*, p. 49.
[18] *Architettura ippodamea*, p. 374.
[19] B. Pace, *Introduzione allo studio dell'archeologia*, Milan 1947, p. 254.
[20] Though, as we have seen, this latter possibility is to be excluded.

part in city planning during the fifth century, both with his practice and through his theories.

Some specific elements of his work can be discussed. The functional orientation with respect to sun and winds has been dealt with. We are reminded of the epithet μετεωρολόγος given him by Hesychius and Photios.

Furthermore, town planning whose architecture is inspired by social principles well agrees with Hippodamus's studies on political constitutions.

Finally, the type of agora that occurs in these regularly patterned cities of the fifth century is, according to Pausanias VI, 24, 2, characteristic of the region from which Hippodamus came. Conversely, the Attic system of planning streets is synonymous with the irregular city: see Philostratus *Apoll.* II, 23 concerning a city in India: ἡ πόλις δ᾽ ὡς μὲν ἔχει τοῦ τείχους, εἴρηκα, φασὶ δ᾽ ὡς ἀτάκτως τε καὶ ᾽Αττικῶς τοὺς στενωποὺς τέτμηται ... (I have already described the way in which the city is walled, but they say that it was divided up into narrow streets in the same irregular manner as is Athens. . . .)

Chapter 4

The Etruscan and
Italic Cities

Axial layouts are found at Veio, possibly at Monterado and Cortona,[1] and certainly in the archaic nucleus of Pompeii (which might be attributed to the Italic environment). Thus it appears that the axial system was not unknown even in the Etrusco–Italic world where, as has been said, it developed independently of Greek influences, at least in its elementary form. The more complex layouts such as those of Capua and Marzabotto, on the other hand, are thought to be the result of direct Greek influence. The orthogonal layout of Veio presented by von Gerkan[2] is undoubtedly pure fantasy and in any case belongs to the Roman epoch, as Lehmann–Hartleben observes.[3] Finally, there is a small sector of Vetulonia with road crossings.[4] This has been highly acclaimed, especially by Patroni,[5] as basic evidence of the Etruscan grid plan and has been compared by him to the plans of Marzabotto and Pompeii. In reality, the remains of Vetulonia, which belong to the late Etruscan and Etrusco–Roman periods, prove the opposite. In no sense can they be considered an example of uniform planning when compared to the perfect orthogonality achieved even in layouts on mountain sites.

The only characteristic of Etruscan city planning that can be documented now, given our present inadequate knowledge, is the axial system, already noted by Haverfield and von Gerkan as being characteristic of the Italic people. Yet we must point out first that the system is also found in Greece, and second that it has no prehistory. Attempts to derive the axial system from the terremare plan failed after it was learned that the terremare did not have a regular plan, nor has it been possible to establish the *cardine* and *decumanus* in Villanovian Bologna.[6]

On the other hand, the axial system, once perfected, found widespread use in the Roman world. It is not found in Rome itself, as Varro supposed: (Solin. I, 17: *dictaque primum est Roma quadrata, quod ad aequilibrium foret posita.* In other words, bounded and delineated by means of the *groma*.) Following Varro's lead several scholars, especially Täubler[7] and Basanoff,[8] have attempted unsuccessfully to reconstruct a *cardine* and *decumanus* on

---

[1] The necropolis of Orvieto is laid out in a regular pattern.
[2] A. von Gerkan, *Griechische Städteanlagen*, Fig. 16.
[3] *Realencyclopaedie* IIIA, c. 2029.
[4] I. Falchi, *Not. Scavi* 1895, p. 272; 1898, p. 83. See D. Levi, *St. Etr.* 5, 1931, p. 21; G. Renzetti, *ibid.* 21, 1950–1951, p. 294.
[5] G. Patroni, "Vetulonia, Pompei e la sua storia," *St. Etr.* 15, 1941, p. 109.
[6] See A. Grenier, "Bologne villanovienne et étrusque," *Bibl. Ec. Franç.* 106, 1912, p. 38.
[7] E. Täubler, "Roma Quadrata und mundus," *Röm. Mitt.* 41, 1926, p. 212, 218.
[8] V. Basanoff, "Pomerium Palatinum," *Mem. Lincei* 6, 9, 1939, p. 3.

the Palatine. Not much more fortunate is Piganiol's attempt to find a *cardine* and *decumanus* through the Roman Forum.[9]

Special significance surrounded the use of the axial system as it was elaborated. For the Etruscans it incorporated the relation between terrestrial delimitation and the celestial *templum*.[10] The heavens were like a circle divided into four parts by two axes. The *cardine* and *decumanus* as employed in city planning were an earthly representation of the heavenly pattern. Further delineations within the four sectors determined the distribution of the seats of the gods (known principally through Martianus Capella). These arrangements within the four sectors were closely tied to the art of reading omens by the quadrant in which lightning is seen and to augury, as seen by the subdivisions of the entrails of Piacenza, inscribed with the names of gods appropriate to each. The various sectors were probably also linked to the flight of birds. The Etruscans, however, unlike the Romans and Umbrians, left no trace of this art.

Thus, to the *templum* of the heavens corresponded a *templum* on earth, that is, the "place consecrated by auspices." Unfortunately,

---

[9] A. Piganiol, "Les origines du Forum," *Mél. Ec. Franç.* 27, 1908, p. 233.

[10] Hyg. Grom. 131 Th.: *Constituti enim limites non sine mundi ratione, quoniam decumani secundum solis decursum diriguntur, kardines a poli axe. Unde primum haec ratio mensurae constituta ab Etruscorum haruspicum disciplina; quod ille orbem terrarum in duas partes secundum solis cursum diviserunt, dextram appellaverunt quae septentrioni subiacebat, sinistram quae ad meridianum terrae esset ⟨ab oriente ad⟩ occasum, quod eo sol et luna spectaret; alteram lineam duxerunt a meridiano in septentrionem et a media ultra antica[m] citra postica[m] nominaverunt. Ex quo haec constitutio liminibus templorum adscribitur.* Front. 10 Th.: *Limitum prima origo, sicut Varro descripsit, a disciplina Etrusca; quod aruspices orbem terrarum in duas partes diviserunt, dextram appellaverunt quae septentrioni subiaceret, sinistram quae a meridiano terra⟨e⟩ esse⟨t⟩ ⟨ab oriente ad⟩ occasum, quod eo sol et luna spectaret, sicut quidam + carpiunt architecti delubra in occidente⟨m⟩ recte spectare scripserunt. Aruspices altera[m] linea[m] a septentrione ad meridianum diviserunt terram, ⟨et⟩ a me[ri]dia[no] ultra antica, citra postica nominaverunt.* See also Hyg. Grom. 134 Th. (The *limites* were established not without consideration for the celestial system, since the *decumani* were laid out according to the sun and the *cardines* according to the celestial axis. This system of measurement for the first time established the teachings of the Etruscans; these indeed divided the earth into two parts according to the course of the sun. The part situated at the north they called right, and that situated toward the south they considered left; from east to west, because the sun and moon are directed in these ways. The other line led from south to north and the parts on the far side of this line they called *antica*, and the parts on this side they called *postica*. And from these terms the boundaries of the temple also came to be described. [Frontinus, 10 Th.] The first origin of the *limites*, as Varro described them, derives from the Etruscan doctrine. Indeed, the *hauspices* (prophesiers) divided the world into two parts; they called "right" that part situated at the north and "left" that part at the south, from east to west because the sun and the moon travel in that way, and for this reason architects have written that it is right that the temples should be oriented toward the west. The *haruspices* divided the earth with a different line, from north to south, and the part on the other side of the line they called *antica* and the part on this side *postica*.)

75

the evidence concerning the orientation of the *templum* is contradictory.[11] Varro, *De Ling. Lat.* VII, 7,[12] Festus 454 L,[13] and Pliny, *Nat. Hist.* II, 143[14] all imply that a southern orientation was preferable. From Livy I, 18, 6,[15] Dionysius of Halicarnassus, *Ant. Rom.* II, 5, 2–3,[16] Plutarch *Quaest. Rom,* 78,[17] Servius *Aen.* II, 693,[18] and Isidorus, *Etym.* XV, 4, 7,[19] we infer an eastern orientation. Yet Vitruvius IV, 5, 1,[20] who according to Nissen[21] draws from Hellenistic sources, recommends that the front of the temple

[11] See especially C. O. Thulin, "Die Etruskische Disciplin, III, Die Ritual-bücher," *Göteborgs Högskolas Årsskrift*, 1909, p. 28; A. L. Frothingam, "Ancient Orientation Unveiled," *Amer. Journ. Archeol.* 21, 1917, p. 55, 187, 313, 420; H. J. Rose, "The Inauguration of Numa," *J. Roman Stud.* 13, 1923, p. 82; S. Weinstock, "Templum," *Röm. Mitt.* 47, 1932, p. 95 (p. 128 for the interpretation of Janus quadrifront); for a discussion of the *templum* and *limitatio* see M. Pallottino, *Etruscologia*, Milan, 1955, p. 210.

[12] . . . *eius templi partes quattuor dicuntur sinistra ab oriente, dextra ab occasu, antica ad meridiem, postica ad septentrionem* . . . (the four parts of the temple are said to be "left," those to the east, "right," those to the west, *antica* toward the south, *postica* toward the north . . .)

[13] *Sinistrae aves sinistrumque e[s]t sinistimum auspicium, id est quod sinat fieri. Varro lib. V Epistolicarum Quaestionum ait: "A deorum sede cum in meridiem spectes, ad sinistram sunt parte⟨s⟩ mundi exorientes, ad dexteram occidentes; factum arbitror, ut sinistra meliora auspicia quam dextra esse existimentur". Idem fere sentiunt Sinnius Capito et Cincius. Paul. Fest. 244 L.: Posticum ostium dicitur in posteriore parte aedium. . . . Denique at quae ante nos sunt antica, et quae post nos sunt postica dicuntur, et dexteram anticam, sinistram posticam dicimus. Sic etiam ea caeli pars, quae sole inlustratur ad meridiem, antica nominatur, quae ad septentrionem, postica; rursumque dividuntur in duas partes, orientem atque occidentem.* (Birds to the left and augury to the left: that is what permits us to act. Varro in the fifth book of the *Epistolicae Questiones* says: "When you look south from the seat of the gods, the east is at your left, the west at your right; I believe it is for this reason that the auguries on the left are thought to be better than those on the right." Sinnius Capito and Cincius are of the same opinion. (Paul. Fest. 244 L.) The door at the back of the house is called the *posticum ostium* . . . and finally the doors that are in front are called *antica* and those behind us *postica*; and we call the right-hand door antique and the left-hand postique. And thus also that part of the heavens that is lit by the sun toward the south we call *antica*, and that toward the north *postica*, and again the sky is divided into two parts, east and west.)

[14] *In sedecim partes coelum in eo spectu divisere Tusci. Prima est a septentrionibus ad aequinoctialem exortum, secunda ad meridiem, tertia ad aequinoctialem occasum, quarta obtinet quod est reliquum ab occasu ad septentriones.* (In making these observations the Tuscans divided the heaven into sixteen parts: the first quarter is from the north to the equinoctial sunrise (east), the second to the south, the third to the equinoctial sunset (west), and the fourth occupies the remaining space extending from west to north . . .)

[15] . . . *ab augure . . . deductus (Numa) in arcem in lapide ad meridiem versus consedit. Augur ad laevam eius capite valato sedem cepit, dextra manu baculum sine nodo aduncum tenens, quem lituum appellarunt. Inde ubi prospectu in urbem agrumque capto deos precatus regiones ab oriente ad occasum determinavit, dextras ad meridiem partes, laevas ad septentrionem esse dixit, signum contra quoad longissime conspectum oculi tenebant, animo finivit* . . . (An augur conducted him to the citadel and caused him to sit down on a stone, facing the south. The augur seated himself on Numa's left, having his head covered, and holding in his right hand the crooked staff without a knot which they call a *lituus*. Then, looking out over the City and the country beyond, he prayed to the gods, and marked off the heavens by a line from east to west, designating as "right" the regions to the south, as "left" those to the north, and fixing in his mind a landmark opposite to him and as far away as the eye could reach . . .)

76

face west. This orientation is the one the *gromatici* knew, for they favored the west not only for the orientation of the temple but especially for base lines for land surveys.[22] And finally, it appears from Homer, *M* 237 ff. and Plato *De Leg.* VI, 760d[23] that the Greeks had a northern orientation. Many different cosmic systems merge in these doctrines and make it almost impossible to point out time sequences, since they range from Babylonian times through to the Hellenistic era.[24] As Cicero observed, the fundamental motive is certainly the quadripartite division of the heavens, which accounts also for the system of sixteen regions.[25] This motive is common in the Babylonian

---

[16]Τίθενται δὲ Ῥωμαῖοι τὰς ἐκ τῶν ἀριστερῶν ἐπὶ τὰ δεξιὰ ἀστραπὰς αἰσίους, εἴτε παρὰ Τυρρηνῶν διδαχθέντες, εἴτε πατέρων καθηγησαμένων κατὰ τοιόνδε τινά, ὡς ἐγὼ πείθομαι, λογισμόν, ὅτι καθέδρα μὲν ἐστι καὶ στάσις ἀρίστη τῶν οἰωνοῖς μαντευομένων ἡ βλέπουσα πρὸς ἀνατολάς ... Τοῖς δὲ πρὸς ἀνατολὰς βλέπουσιν ἀριστερὰ μὲν γίνεται τὰ πρὸς τὴν ἄρκτον ἐπιστρέφοντα μέρη, δεξιὰ δὲ τὰ πρὸς μεσημβρίαν φέροντα· τιμιώτερα δὲ τὰ πρότερα πέφυκεν εἶναι τῶν ὑστέρων. (Now the Romans look upon the lightning that passes from the left to the right as a favorable omen, having been thus instructed either by the Tyrrhenians or by their own ancestors. Their reason is, in my opinion, that the best seat and station for those who take the auspices is that which looks toward the east ... Now to those who look toward the east the parts facing toward the north are on the left and those extending toward the south are on the right, and the former are by nature more honorable than the latter.)
[17]'Διὰ τί τῶν οἰωνῶν ὁ καλούμενος ἀριστερὸς αἴσιος;' ... Ἢ μᾶλλον, ὡς Ἰόβας φησί, τοῖς πρὸς τὰς ἀνατολὰς ἀποβλέπουσιν ἐν ἀριστερᾷ γίνεται τὸ βόρειον, ὃ δὴ τοῦ κόσμου δεξιὸν ἔνιοι τίθενται καὶ καθυπέρτερον; (Why of birds is the one called "left-hand" a bird of good omen ... or is it rather, as Juba declares, that as anyone looks eastward, the north is on the left, and some make out the north to be the right, or upper, side of the universe?)
[18] ... *sinistras autem partes septentrionales esse augurum disciplina consentit.* ... (... the teaching of the augurers establishes that the northern zones are left. ...)
[19] ... *locus designatus ad orientem a contemplatione templum dicebatur. Cuius partes quattuor erant, antica ad ortum, postica ad occasum, sinistra ad septentrionem, dextra ad meridiem spectans.* ... (... the place designated toward the east was said to be for contemplation, the *templum*. Four parts did it have: that toward the east *antica*, *postica* that toward the west; the northern part left, and the southern part right. ...)
[20]*Regiones autem quas debent spectare aedes sacrae deorum immortalium sic erunt constituendae uti si nulla ratio impedierit liberaque fuerit potestas, aedis signumque quod erit in cella conlocatum spectet ad vespertinam caeli regionem, uti qui adierint ad aram immolantes aut sacrificia facientes spectent ad partem caeli orientis et simulacrum quod erit in aede.* ... (The aspects which the sacred temples of the immortal gods ought to regard are so to be appointed (if no reason hinders, and the opportunity is presented) that the temple and the statue which is in the shrine look toward the western quarter of the sky, so that those who come to the altar to sacrifice or make offerings may look toward the eastern heaven and the image in the temple. ...)
[21]*Orientation* II, p. 113.
[22]See footnote 10.
[23]The contradiction among the various systems has already been noted by Arnobius, *Adv. gent.* IV, 5.
[24]See in particular S. Weinstock, "Martianus Capella and the Cosmic System of the Etruscans," *J. Roman Stud.* 36, 1946, p. 101.
[25]Cicero, *De divin.* II, 42: ... *coelum in sedicim partes diviserunt Etrusci. Facile id quidem fuit, quattuor quas nos habemus duplicare, post idem iterum facere, ut ex eo dicerent fulmen qua ex parte venisset.* ... (... the Etruscans divided the heavens into sixteen parts. Indeed, it was easy to double the four parts that we have, and then to repeat that same multiplication, in order to determine the part from whence comes the thunder. ...)

art of speculation as a function of augury[26] and probably derives from it.[27] Changes in the art of orientation reflect differences in ritual. The Etruscans, however, did favor a southerly orientation. Aside from the authority of Varro and the other sources cited by Festus (see footnote 13), the orientation of the Comitium Romanus, with the Curia to the north and the Tribunal to the south,[28] can be adduced as evidence. The Saepta Iulia which supposedly follow a more ancient layout are also on a north–south axis. South-facing temples were the most common. This orientation was precise at Marzabotto, the Temple of Apollo in Rome, and at Jupiter Anxur at Terracina (though its terrace did not comply) but was only approximate at Civitacastellana, Bolsena, the Capitolium at Rome, and at Segni. Frequently the urban pattern prevailed over the religious one. The Greek temples, on the other hand, faced east as a matter of principle.

Theories of Surveyors

In the cities and in the *agri centuriati*, the orientation system is different. The base line here is east–west. There is no doubt that the doctrines of the *gromatici* are abstract speculations that have artificially superimposed cosmic theories on standard surveying practice. However, it appears exaggerated to believe that these doctrines were formulated by Varro, based on the Hellenistic theories of westerly orientation of the temples, as Barthel maintains.[29] Nor can we say, as Weinstock maintains,[30] that there was no link between the art of surveying and the theories of the cosmos. Contrary to the usual statements, there are examples of oriented centuriation;[31] it must also be noted that the centuriation was designed after the *groma* with auspices had been placed.

Having made these qualifications, we must nevertheless agree in relating the theorizing of the *gromatici* to the erudition of the late Republic. In particular, the system of urban and agrarian delimitation has nothing in common with the *templum*, as is seen even in the fact of east–west orientation rather than north–south. (However, W. Müller maintains that a relation existed

[26] By means of observing lightning (and winds and rainbows. See M. Jastrow, *Die Religion Babyloniens und Assyriens*, 2nd ed., II, Giessen, 1912, p. 705). Quadripartition was found in Greece in the system of Octotropos: see Weinstock, "Martianus Capella."
[27] See footnote 47.
[28] See *Doxa* 3, 1950, p. 69 (though many differ, among them A. von Gerkan, *Rend. Acc. Napoli* 21, 1941, p. 263).
[29] *Bonn. Jahrb.* 120, 1911, p. 115. Also Fabricius, Pauly–Wissowa, *Realencylopaedie* 13, c. 685.
[30] *J. Roman Stud.* 1946, p. 129.
[31] For example see ager Campanus (though it has a north–south *decumanus*) Cesena, Bologna, Cremona, and Pavia.

between the *templum* of the augurs and the use of delimitation, and he sees delimitation as a transposition of an ancient concept of the celestial calendar.[32])

But it is the city that interests us particularly. The theories of K. O. Müller and Nissen of a city being a *templum* have been justly denied by Valeton[33] and by Thulin.[34] Although the founding of the city occurred according to an Etruscan ritual,[35] *inauguratio urbis* dealt with tracing the walls, not with patterning the city itself, as Valeton observes.[36] The theory of Kornemann,[37] must be reconsidered with skepticism. He compares the distinctive character of the *urbs* to the *oppidum* in the sacred delimitation of the *templum* and in the confines of the *pomerium*. Likewise, there is much doubt about an element always considered fundamental to the supposed urban *templum*, and that is the *mundus* in the city center. At Ostia, Calza[38] for one proposes to find the *mundus* at the crossing of the *cardine* and *decumanus*. However, if there is any one thing clear from the texts, as Hedlund[39] especially has shown, it is that the *mundus* has nothing to do with the rites of founding the city.[40] In fact, the *mundus* at Rome was a cavern sacred to Ceres and the Mani, and there is no source that places it on the Palatine.

Mundus

A further line of reasoning in favor of the relationship between

Theory of the Quadripartite Circle

[32] W. Müller, *Kreis und Kreuz*, Berlin, 1938.
[33] *Mnemos.* 21, 1893, p. 65.
[34] Thulin, *Die Etruskische Disciplin*.
[35] Festus 358 L: *Rituales nominantus Etruscorum libri, in quibus perscribtum est, quo ritu condantur urbes, arae, aedes sacrentur, qua sanctitate muri, quo iure portae, quomodo tribus, curiae, centuriae distribuantur, exercitus constituantur, ordinentur. . . .* Cf. Varro, *L. L.* V, 143; Livy I, 44, 3; Plutarch, *Rom.* 11; Macr. *Sat.* V, 19, 13. (The books of the Etruscans are called rituals, within which is prescribed the ceremony of founding the city, and of consecrating the altars and temples. Those books according to which the walls are built are called religious, and where one finds the standards for building the gates, the modes in which the tribes are distributed, the centuriations, the curiae that are formed and ordered for the armies. . . .)
[36] Confirmation of Valeton's arguments is to be found in the fact that the sacred area *Roma Quadrata* (Festus 310 L.) *ubi reposita sunt quae solent boni ominis gratia in urbe condenda adhiberi* (where are placed the things that one is accustomed to use as good auguries in the foundation of a city) was not at the center of the Palatine, as current opinion would have it, but most probably as I have proposed (*Studies Robinson* I, p. 389) along the periphery of the city (as Festus himself says, *ante templum Apollinis*), and is one and the same with the pit, later covered with an altar, from which Romulus began to furrow (Ov. *Fasti* IV, 819).
[37] E. Kornemann, "Polis und Urbs," *Klio* 15, 1915, p. 78.
[38] *Scavi di Ostia* I, p. 70.
[39] Y. Hedlund, "Mundus," *Eranos* 31, 1933, p. 53. See also the observations made by H. J. Rose, "The Mundus," *Studi e Mater. St. Relig.* 7, 1931, p. 115. See also *Studies Robinson* I, p. 389.
[40] An obvious erudite construct is the *mundus* of the Comitium in Plutarch *Rom.* 11.

the *templum* and the city has been set forth—namely the theory
of a quadripartite circular city analogous to the Oriental city,
postulated on two basic arguments. The first, concerning the
circular form in general, is based on the morphological link
between *urbs* and *orbis*,[41] already established by Varro but without
foundation.[42] The second argument, advanced by W. Müller[43]
among others, is that the appellative *Roma quadrata* should be
taken to mean quadripartite, as Altheim had formerly proposed,
and that the concept of a circular city is to be found in a passage
of Plutarch.[44] The difficulty here is that, even if this interpretation of *quadrata* is valid, it must be explained in some other way.[45]
Furthermore, the reference from Plutarch concerns a theory
that has nothing to do with *Roma quadrata*; in fact, the passage
has no value even as testimony to a tradition of a circular Rome.[46]

In conclusion, the celestial *templum* and the augurial *templum*
are distinct from urban road patterning systems. For the systems
of orienting the temple, the following choronological references
exist: on the evidence of Saepta Iulia, probably the fourth century; and on the evidence of the Comitium and the Temple of
Jupiter, the end of the sixth century, although a much older date
can be assigned to the art of divination, especially if we allow
ties with the East by way of Mesopotamia.[47]

Greek Influence

On the other hand, the orientation of the city, later employed
in the *agri divisi*, is attributable to Greek influence, especially on
the grounds of the Greek origin of the word *groma*, as Thulin has
suggested.[48] Posidonia can be adduced as additional evidence,
since it is an example of east–west orientation.

These conclusions substantially diminish the importance of the

[41] See H. Herter, *Rhein. Mus.* 96, 1953, p. 5.
[42] For *urbs* see G. Devoto, *St. Etr.* XV, p. 147.
[43] W. Müller, *Kreis und Kreuz*, Berlin 1938, p. 59.
[44] Plutarch *Rom.* 11: Ὁ δὲ Ῥωμύλος ... ὤκιζε τὴν πόλιν ... Βόθρος γὰρ ὠρύγη περὶ τὸ νῦν
Κομίτιον κυκλοτερής ... Εἶθ' ὥσπερ κύκλον κέντρῳ περιέγραψαν τὴν πόλιν.
(Romulus . . . founded the city . . . a circular ditch was dug around the place
where now the comitium is. . . . Then the city was laid out like a circle around
a center.)
[45] See *Studies Robinson* I, p. 389.
[46] Circular Rome with its center at the Comitium is an elaborate reconstruction
based upon the circular plan city as presented by Varro. It is comparable to
those cities that have a central forum. Possibly the theory developed from the
umbilicus urbis, placed at the comitium, analogous to the ομφαλοί located at the
agora of Greek cities (or as seen from Plato's history of Atlantis, as Blumenthal
would believe, *Klio* 35, 1942, p. 181, no. 3).
[47] The relationship with the Near East is widely discussed: see in particular
R. Pettazzoni, "Elementi extraitalici nella divinazione etrusca," *St. Etr.* I,
p. 195; G. Furlani, "Epatoscopia babilonese ed epatoscopia etrusca," *Studi
e mater. di St. delle Relig.* 4, 1928, p. 243.
[48] *Die Etruskische Disciplin* III, p. 30.

80

Etruscan influence upon the development of uniformly planned cities. Only after the fourth century do certain original developments emerge. Two fundamental characteristics of Etruscan–Italic architecture can be singled out, orthogonality and axial symmetry (which the Etruscans are supposed to have inherited in turn from the Egyptian–Mesoptamian world).[49] These characteristics are found in the layouts of temples, houses, and towns. It is not correct, however, to claim that these characteristics are exclusively Etruscan, particularly if the axial house plan is of Eastern derivation, as seems likely.[50] Nor can we ignore that Etruscan and Italic influence in the development of the regular city was slight. As Pallottino has noted, frontality and axial symmetry pertain to the entire Mediterranean culture.

[49] See especially G. Kaschnitz-Weinberg, "Vergleichende Studien zur italisch-römischen Struktur," *Röm. Mitt.* 59, 1944, p. 89; A. Boethius, *Roman and Greek Town Architecture*; E. Gjerstad, "Die Ursprungsgeschichte der römischen Kaiserfora," *Acta Inst. Rom. Regni Sueciae* 10, 1944, p. 40, especially p. 68; M. Pallottino, "Giudizi e pregiudizi sull'architettura italica," *Archeol. Class.* I, 1949, p. 196.
[50] E. Gjerstad, "The Palace at Vouni," *Acta Inst. Rom. Regni Sueciae* 2, 1932, p. 145.

Chapter 5

**Greek Cities of the Fourth
Century B.C. and in the
Hellenistic Era**

Cnidus	The use of the grid plan, with emphasis of the *per strigas* subdivision, continues after the fifth century B.C. The blocks of Cnidus,[1] dating perhaps from the fourth century B.C., measure the same as those of Miletus, calculated at 29.50 by 51.60 meters.
Priene	Priene,[2] founded during the second half of the fourth century, has blocks that are more nearly square (35.40 by 47.20 meters or 120 by 160 ft, a ratio of 3:4). The major axes run east–west.
Palairos	In a regularly patterned sector of Palairos[3] dating from the fourth century one finds rectangular blocks with sides in a ratio of 1:2, contained between two wide *decumani* oriented almost exactly east–west, with a series of narrow transverse streets.
Kos	Kos,[4] except for the western sector, is regularly patterned and uniformly subdivided. The center of the city is divided by a *decumanus* 10.50 meters wide, running perfectly east–west. A pattern of *cardines* can be reconstructed from the excavations or from the surviving topography. To the north, in particular, rectangular blocks averaging 100 feet across (25, 31, 35 m) have been excavated, with the long axis running north–south. They are over 52 meters long. The streets measure 4.20, 4.20, 3.40, 8.80, and 3.00 meters in width. We thus have a major *cardine* and four minor ones, or rather a πλατεῖα and four στενωποί, as at Pompeii and supposedly at Thurii. The master plan of Kos, according to Morricone, dates from 366 B.C.
Magnesia	Magnesia on the Maeander River[5] (fourth century B.C.) is patterned on blocks of 42.40 by 98.50 meters, a ratio of 4:9, with streets 5 meters wide.
Soluntum	Soluntum (Fig. 27) is among the better known and more diversely interpreted examples of uniform planning. The city is usually assigned to the Roman era (Cultrera et al.). More precisely, Ferri[6] proposes a date between the end of the second century and the beginning of the first century B.C., based on information from archeological findings. Cavallari and Pace observe that the present layout probably follows the plan of the ancient city, since no differing orientation from an earlier time has been found.[7] Especially because of their common Punic origin, Soluntum and

[1] Von Gerkan, *Griechische Städteanlagen*, p. 92.
[2] T. Wiegand and H. Schrader, *Priene*, Berlin, 1904.
[3] F. Noack, *Arch. Anz.* 1916, c. 221, Fig. 2.
[4] L. Morricone, *Boll. Arte* 35, 1950, p. 70, 220, 234, 319.
[5] C. Humann and J. Kohte, *Magnesia am Meander*, Berlin, 1904.
[6] S. Ferri, "Il problema archeologico di Solunto," *Le Arti* 4, 1941–42, p. 250.
[7] B. Pace, *Arte e civiltà della Sicilia antica* II, p. 365.

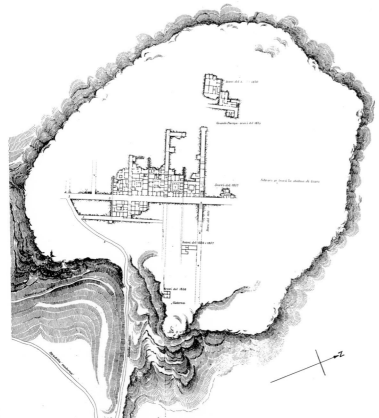

Figure 27 Solunto (Cavallari).

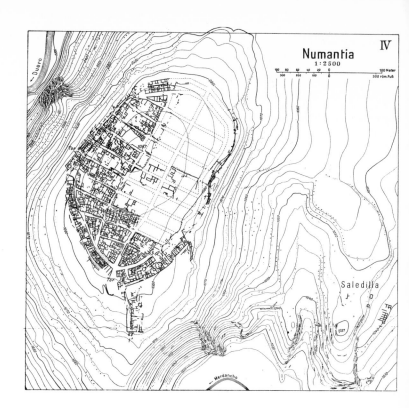

Figure 28 Numantia (Schulten).

Figure 29 Tripoli (Aurigemma).

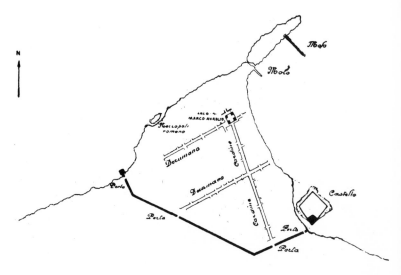

Selinus have been considered to be of a single type, while the Carthaginians are often thought to be the bridge carrying over the uniform planning of the East. Because of this, the plan of Soluntum takes on a particular interest, but there is really no reason to consider it apart from the other regular-plan cities of the Greek world. Here too there is a basic longitudinal axis about 8 meters wide, and rectangular blocks approximately 32 meters wide are marked by the usual series of *cardines*. As at Olynthus, the blocks are bisected lengthwise by an ambitus (0.80 to 1.00 m across) which carries a drainage canal.[8] Instead of being Phoenician or Roman in origin, Soluntum probably should be considered as part of the Greek world, at least until new excavations bring greater certainty.[9]

The same form, a major *decumanus* intersected by a series of *cardines*, is followed in the layout of Tindari.[10] The original plan dates back to the fourth and third centuries B.C.

Tindari

The city recently excavated on the island of Lipari is from the Hellenistic period.[11] It is patterned on a grid of *cardines* about 30 meters apart.

Lipari

This scheme is found in Spain and Sardinia as well. The hypothetical plan, based on the present layout, shows Olbia (Sardinia),[12] dating to the Punic period of the fourth century, to have developed along three strips of rectangular blocks, much elongated, separated by two roads.

Olbia

Numantia, first thought to be a Roman city and later ascertained to be of Iberic origin, has rectangular blocks 23 meters (80 feet) wide whose length is between $2\frac{1}{2}$ and 4 times the width (Fig. 28). Schulten[13] thinks it was built no earlier than 400 B.C. He notes that other Iberian cities, such as Vega de Arienzo and Citania de Briteiros in Portugal follow similar plans.

Numantia

Two large parallel *decumani* 300 meters apart[14] are still apparent in present-day Oea (Tripoli).[15] Though Oea is thought to date

Tripoli

---

[8] *Ibid.*, p. 346 (a further example of the use of the ambitus is found at Mozthya).
[9] *Arch. Anz.* 59, 1954, c. 704.
[10] *Ibid.*, c. 613, Fig. 77.
[11] *Ibid.*, c. 513.
[12] D. Panedda, *Olbia*, Rome, 1952, topographic chart (see p. 12 for the date).
[13] A. Schulten, *Numantia* II, Munich, 1931, p. 134; see also, by the same author, *Geschichte von Numantia*, Munich 1933, Table IV.
[14] The first of these is Sciara Hara el Chebira—Sciara el Cuasc; the second, Sciara Homet Garian.
[15] S. Aurigemma, *Notiz. Archeol.* II, p. 219, Table VIII, A.

from the fourth or third century, the exact date of its founding is unknown (Fig. 29).

Alexandria

The same scheme is continued throughout the Hellenistic era. The character and extent of the plan of Alexandria[16] are in doubt, though the city was probably patterned along three major longitudinal axes parallel to the coast. The land parcels thus created were in turn subdivided into rectangular blocks by perpendicular streets. Some of the streets are very close together, thus creating much-elongated blocks.

Tebtunis

The twelfth-dynasty Egyptian city of Tebtunis (Fig. 30) was reconstructed in 300 B.C., with rectangular blocks on a north–south axis, with also a major east–west street.[17] The irregularity of several of the central sections is due to the merging of the new plan with the old, as at Pompeii.

Smyrna

Smyrna, in the new plan attributed to Antigonus and later to Lysimachus, was laid out on an orthogonal grid (Strabo, XIV, 646: Ἔστι δ’ ἡ ῥυμοτομία διάφορος ἐπ’ εὐθειῶν εἰς δύναμιν (The division into streets is excellent, in straight lines as far as possible), taking διάφορος to mean "excellent" and not "different").[18]

Thessalonica

It is hard to know whether Thessalonica should be included in this category. As shown by Tafrali's reconstruction,[19] the Byzantine city is divided into three wide sectors by two roads, Via Egnazia and Via S. Demetrius (420 meters or 12 actus apart). In the present city there are several streets at right angles to these. It cannot be ascertained whether the subdivision was *per strigas* or based upon square plots, nor whether the Byzantine city dates back to the original plan of the city's foundation in 316 or 315 B.C.[20]

Nicaea

In this context of uniform grid plans, Nicaea is an exception, this city is divided in the middle by two central axes, *decumanus*

---

[16] F. Noack, *Athen. Mitt.* 25, 1900, p. 215; E. Breccia, *Alexandrea ad Aegyptum*, Bergamo, 1922; von Gerkan, *Griechische Städteanlagen*, p. 67, 91.

[17] C. Anti, "Un esempio di sistemazione urbanistica nel III secolo a. C.," *Architettura e Arti Decorative* 10, 1930–1931, p. 97.

[18] As would be translated by Bürchner, Pauly–Wissowa, *Realencyclopaedie* III A, c. 753; Fabricius, *ibid.* III A, c. 1998. See also von Gerkan, *Griechische Städteanlagen*, p. 120.

[19] O. Tafrali, *Topographie de Thessalonique*, Paris, 1912; Pauly–Wissowa, also by the same author; H. von Schoenebeck, "Die Stadtplanung des römischen Thessalonike," *Bericht VI Intern. Kongress*, Berlin, 1940, p. 478.

[20] Schoenebeck's attribution of the plan to the Augustan era is based on insufficient data. A regular pattern is found in the reconstructed layout of Afrodisia in Caria, which however is attributed to the Romans by L. Crema, *Mon. Linc.* 38, 1939, c. 306.

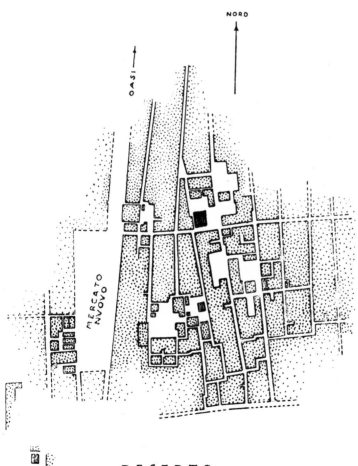

Figure 30 Tebtunis (Anti).

NORD

OASI

NUOVO MERCATO

DESERTO

METRO
0   25   50   75   100

89

and *cardine*, and thus is more Roman than Greek. (The first recorded example is Ostia.) First erected by Antigonus in 316 B.C. and later refounded by Lysimachus, Nicaea of Bithynia is described by Strabo XII, 565: Ἔστι δὲ τῆς πόλεως ἐκκαιδεκαστάδιος ὁ περίβολος ἐν τετραγώνῳ σχήματι· ἔστι δὲ καὶ τετράπυλος ἐν πεδίῳ κείμενος ἐρρυμοτομημένος πρὸς ὀρθὰς γωνίας, ὥστ' ἀφ' ἑνὸς λίθου κατὰ μέσον ἱδρυμένου τὸ γυμνάσιον τὰς τέτταρας ὁρᾶσθαι πύλας. (The city is sixteen stadia in circuit and quadrangular in shape; it is situated in a plain, and has four gates; and its streets are cut at right angles, so that the four gates can be seen from one stone which is set up in the middle of the gymnasium.)

From this passage the following characteristics emerge: a square perimeter, four gates, rectilinear streets and visibility of these gates from one point (either inside or outside the gymnasium).[21] Thus there must have been a central intersection of the two major axes. To exclude the influence of a Roman plan, as von Gerkan has done, appears too labored.[22] However, as Fabricius[23] has noted, some doubt remains whether Strabo saw the original plan or only a later reconstruction of the city under Roman influence.

Hieropolis

At Hieropolis of Phrygia[24] (second century B.C.) the blocks measure 44 by 59 meters (150 by 200 feet), a ratio of 3:4.

Syrian Cities

The regular plan was employed in the layout of the new Seleucid towns of Syria,[25] as Sauvaget has shown through various reconstructions of the ancient plans as traced in the modern cities. The probability that these plans belong to the original foundation of the cities and not to the later Roman rebuilding is borne out by the fact that the Seleucid cities are not only similar among themselves but also similar to other Hellenistic cities. The plan of Dura Europos (Fig. 31), from the first Seleucid period, is known through its ruins. Antioch on the Orontes (Fig. 32), Seleucia of Priene, Apamea on the Orontes, and Laodicea on the sea (Fig. 33) were founded by Seleucos I

[21] See Fabricius, Pauly–Wissowa, *Realencyclopaedie* III A, c. 1998.
[22] *Griechische Städteanlagen*, p. 84.
[23] See footnote 21.
[24] *Jahrbuch, Ergänzungsh.* 4, Table p. 202.
[25] J. Weulersse, "Antioche," *Bull. d'Etudes Orientales*, 4, 1934, p. 27; J. Sauvaget, "Esquisse d'une histoire de la ville de Damas," *Revue des Etudes Islamiques* 4, 1934, p. 422; and "Le plan de Laodicée-sur-mer," *Bull. d'Etudes Orientales*," 1934, p. 81 (for Apamea see p. 94) (reissued in *Memorial J. Sauvaget*, I, Damascus, 1954, p. 101); and *Alep*, Paris, 1941, p. 40, Table 52; also "Le plan antique de Damas," *Syria* 26, 1949, p. 314; *The excavations at Dura Europos, Ninth Season*, I, New Haven, 1944, p. 23, Fig. 12 (F. E. Brown). J. Lauffray gave a paper on *L'Urbanisme antique en proche Orient* at the Second International Congress of Classical Studies, Copenhagen 1954.

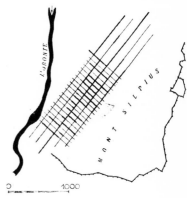

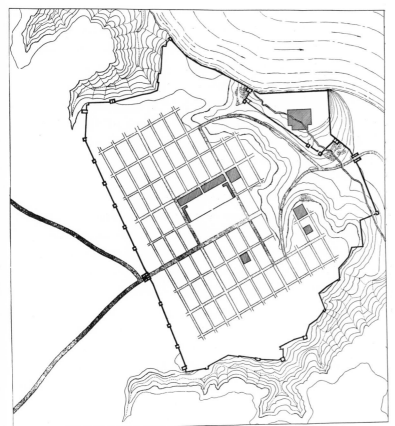

Figure 31 Dura Europos
(*Excavations at Dura Europos*).

Figure 32 Antioch.

0   1000 M.

Figure 33 Laodicea on the Sea.

91

(312–281 B.C.). The enlargement of Aleppo (Beroea) dates from the same period (Fig. 34). Damascus (Fig. 35) was probably rebuilt in the third century B.C.

These cities are marked by a central *decumanus* (that in Dura Europos is 12.67 meters wide)[26] or by several parallel *decumani* (two in Damascus, three in Laodicea) running east–west[27] (Laodicea, Aleppo) or nearly so (Damascus, Dura Europos. Antioch is an exception). These roads are cut by *cardines*, some of which may be wider than others. The short side of the blocks faces the arteries. Roughly equal dimensions occur in all the cities: 58 by 112 meters (almost 200 by 400 feet) at Laodicea and Antioch, about 45 by 119 meters (150 by 400 feet) at Aleppo, 45 by 100 meters at Damascus, and 35.20 by 70.40 meters (120 by 240 feet)[28] at Dura Europos.[29]

H. Lacoste in a personal communication writes that Apamea is patterned on three east–west *decumani* 1500 feet apart. Between these and parallel to them run three minor *decumani*. A major *cardine* 72 feet wide divides the city in a north–south direction, 180 by 360 feet, with their long axes almost invariably perpendicular to the *decumanus*.

Gerasa[30] follows the typical layout, however: two *decumani* cut by one *cardine*. Although it was founded in the first half of the second century, we do not know whether the present plan dates from that time.

One of the last echoes of the city patterned *per strigas* is Taxila (Fig. 36),[31] founded by the Bactrian Greeks in the early years of the second century B.C. between the Indus and the Jhelum rivers.

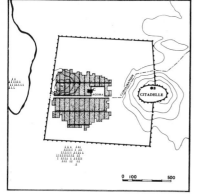

Figure 34 Beroea.

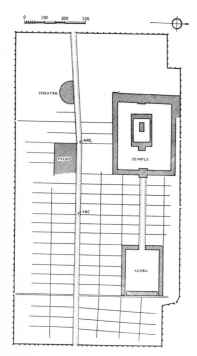

Figure 35 Damascus (Sauvaget).

[26] The others measure 6.33 meters and 8.45 meters.
[27] The development and growth of these arteries usually occurs along the longitudinal axis; Laodicea is an exception because of the particular configuration of the site.
[28] Brown in *Excavations at Dura Europos*, p. 24, establishes the equivalence as 100 by 200 feet at 0.352 meters per foot.
[29] Other common characteristics of these cities include the arcades along the main artery and the acropolis sited along the perimeter walls.
[30] C. H. Kraeling, *Gerasa*, New Haven, 1938, p. 14, Table 1.
[31] J. Marshall, *Taxila*, Cambridge, 1951. Figure 36 is reproduced from Table 10 of the third volume.

Figure 36 Taxila (Marshall).

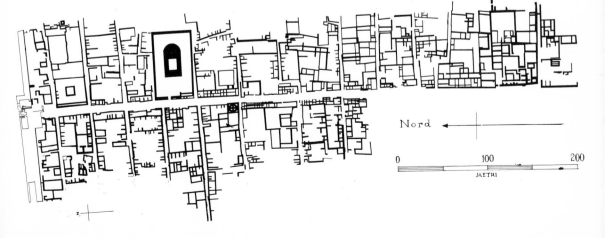

Nord

0   100   200

METRI

Chapter 6

Roman Cities

Hippodamean Type

The Romans used more than one type of city plan, and it is thus not possible to contrast a Greek plan with a Roman one. We will consider first the type characterized by a rectangular grid derived directly from the Hippodamean city, Norba is the most ancient example of this type.

Norba

At the turn of the century Norba was thoroughly studied by L. Savignoni and R. Mengarelli.[1] Their excavations along the perimeter walls and among the temples established these as dating from the fourth century B.C. The plan of the city which arose from this work clearly shows the location of the acropolis and the walls but disregards the rest. The perfect orthogonality of the system can be seen from the aerial photograph (Fig. 37).

Norba was built up of terraces buttressed by a system of walls that were almost always parallel and perpendicular to each other. The city is an interesting example of an urbanism that exploits the difficulties of the terrain to obtain striking results. From the lower portions of the city one viewed the rising terraces, culminating with the Great Acropolis at the central peak. This was a vast terrace perfectly incorporated in the general scheme. On the axis of this terrace, in the center of the city, is a larger, more recent building with a cistern. To the south of the acropolis some blocks still remain, one actus wide, separated by streets four meters wide. The task of future excavations, aside from ascertaining the system of the terraces, would be to explore the road pattern to determine the nature of the grid system. It is possible that a longitudinal road exists at right angles to the long axis of the blocks.

It is impossible to separate the chronology of the city plan from that of the walls and acropolis. Excluding the foundation of the colony in 499 B.C., such a complete rebuilding of the city could have occurred after the incursions of the Privernati in 342 B.C. (Livy VII, 42, 8) or during or after the Privernate war when the Monti Lepini were occupied.[2]

Alba Fucens

Notwithstanding the difficulties of planning and building on mountainous terrain, Alba Fucens[3] is formed on an orthogonal pattern of streets (Fig. 38). This became apparent after recent

[1] *Not. Scavi* 1901, p. 514; 1903, p. 229; 1904, p. 403; see *Atti Congr. Int. Scienze Storiche* 5, Rome, 1904, p. 255. (The article *Norba* in the *Realencyclopaedie*, 1936, ignores the research work of Savignoni and Mengarelli.) See also Blake, *Ancient Roman Construction*, p. 96.
[2] Such is the date given in Lugli, "Le fortificazioni delle antiche città italiche," *Rend. Lincei* 8, 2, 1947, p. 297.
[3] See in particular J. Mertens, *Antiquité Classique* 23, 1954, p. 77.

96

Figure 37 Aerial view of Norba
(Istituto Geografico Mil.).

Figure 38 Alba Fucens (Mertens).

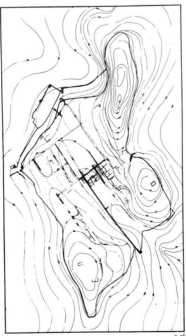

excavations by a Belgian party. Founded as a colony in 303 B.C., it follows wide longitudinal axes cut by minor transverse streets[4] that delimit blocks one actus wide and more than double that figure in length. The blocks are arranged with their long side parallel to the logitudinal axis (*decumanus*). This is a new expression of the Hippodamean plan, patterned by *scamna* and not *per strigas* (if the term *scamna* may be borrowed from the vocabulary of the military encampments and agrarian surveys). This system must have been preferred for its adaptability to the terrain. No precedents are known to exist, though later cities followed similar practice.

Cosa

The work which the American Academy in Rome[5] has carried out at Cosa in the last few years has contributed greatly to the study of regular planning systems. Cosa, a colony founded in 273 B.C. (Fig. 39), presents a strong orthogonal pattern notwithstanding the difficulties of the terrain. Thus Norba, Alba, and Cosa contradict the theory that regular patterning could be applied only to the cities in the plains.[6] It is difficult to single out a main *cardine* and *decumanus* at Cosa, although the road system[7] subdivides the city into rectangular blocks in the center of the city, 32.50 to 37 meters wide (1 actus) and usually more than twice as long (82 meters between K and O streets).

Benevento

Detailed research could ascertain whether Benevento (268 B.C.) was also patterned by elongated rectangles such as we see in the modern plan, one actus wide and uniformly arranged on a north–south axis.

Faleri Novi

At Faleri Novi, too (apparently somewhat later than 241 B.C.) there is a regular pattern, as is apparent in Lugli's reconstruction.[8] Rectangular blocks can perhaps be discerned, one actus wide and placed on the principal axis, which is oriented east–west.

Modena

On the other hand, Haverfield is in error when he attributes to the Roman age that section of Modena which has very long and narrow blocks.[9] The ancient nucleus is found instead to the east

---

[4]The first measure 3.60–3.80 meters (*decumanus maximus*); 2.40 m., 5.35 m.; the *cardine maximus* measures 3.30–3.76 meters.
[5]F. E. Brown, "Cosa I," *Mem. Amer. Acad.* 20, 1951, especially p. 24.
[6]See Lehmann–Hartleben, *Realencyclopaedie* IIIA, c. 2043.
[7]The main streets are between 5.90 and 6.20 meters wide, the secondary streets 4.45 meters wide.
[8]G. Lugli, *La tecnica edilizia in Roma e nel Lazio*, in press. See also Lehmann–Hartleben, *Realencyclopaedie* IIIA, c. 2044.
[9]*Ancient Town-Planning*, p. 69; the scheme is compared to the VI region of Pompeii.

Figure 39 Cosa (Brown).

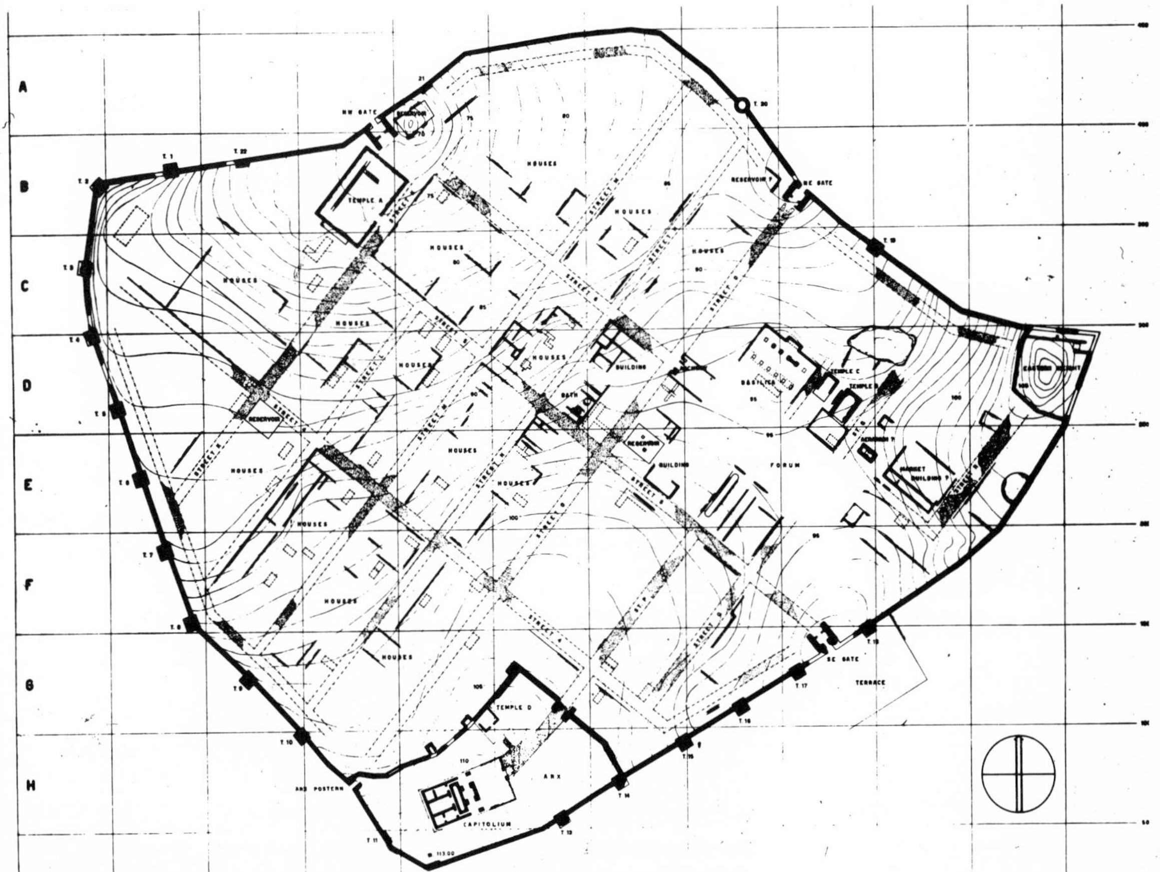

99

of this sector, as is recognized by both Lehmann–Hartleben[10] and Corradi–Cervi.[11]

We should remember that during this same era the Italian cities of Greek origin were completing their master plans, following the Hippodamean pattern (Pompeii, Soluntum, Agrigento). Even second-century Rome had an example of *strigae*. A block excavated in Via Nazionale near Villa Aldobrandini was 35 meters wide and 58.30 meters (about 200 feet) long.[12]

Cities Based on Intersection of Central Axes

Ostia

Of exceptional importance in the context of Roman planning is the city of early Ostia, the plan of which is known today through special studies and through the publication of the excellent first volume reporting the excavations (Fig. 40).[13]

Ostia's origin has been attributed to the last decade of the fourth century B.C. for archeological reasons (architectural terra cottas) and for historical congruity (the need to control the sea after the fall of Anzio).[14] The city follows a regular plan (193.94 by 125.70 meters), divided into four equal sectors by two orthogonal axes which intersect at the center of the city. These axes can be termed *cardine* and *decumanus*[15] by analogy to the techniques of surveying. The orientation is dictated by the axis of the river.

Thus begins a city type characteristically Roman, followed and developed through many colonies. This type is defined as *castrum* in comparison with the fortress cities of the Imperial era. We speak of the *castrum* of Ostia. However, the term is not exact if we consider the plan of contemporary military encampments, which have an entirely different scheme of internal division. Frontinus excludes any imitation of the encampments, *Strat.* IV, 1, 14, by his evidence that camps were not employed before the time of Pyrrhus.[16]

Minturno

The plan of the oldest part of Minturno (Fig. 41) is very similar to that of Ostia, even in dimensions.[17] It is a rectangle of about 182 by 155 meters. (Excavations of the walls on the west and the

[10]*Realencyclopaedie* IIIA, c. 2045.

[11]M. Corradi-Cervi, "Mutina," *R. Deputaz. di Storia Patria per l'Emilia e la Romagna, Sez. Modena, Studi e documenti* I, 1937, p. 137.

[12]*Bull. Com.* 4, 1876, p. 102, Tables XVI–XVII.

[13]*Scavi di Ostia* I, Rome, 1953, p. 75 (Calza); p. 93 (Becatti).

[14]But Säflund does not consider this date probable. (*Le Mura di Roma repubblicana*, Lund 1932, p. 240.)

[15]Width 7.35 and 6.90 meters, respectively.

[16]See footnote 71, p. 120.

[17]J. Johnson, *Excavations at Minturnae* I, Philadelphia 1935, p. 1 (see p. 16, 78 for the *aedes Iovis*); S. Aurigemma, A. De Santis, *Gaeta Formia Minturno*, Rome 1955, p. 41.

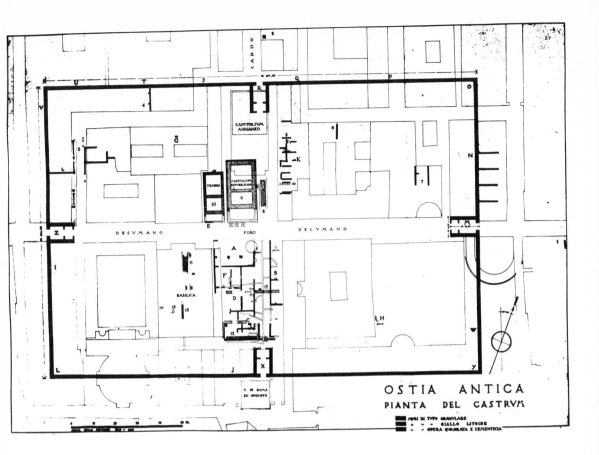

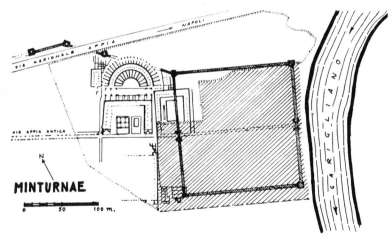

Figure 40 Ostia (*Scavi di Ostia*).

Figure 41 Minturno (Aurigemma–De Santis).

beginnings of those on the adjacent sides testify to these dimensions.) The layout was oriented not exactly to the north but on the axis of the Liri; the Via Appia cut the city in half, constituting the *decumanus*, and we can presume that there was a *cardine* intersecting at right angles at the center. This part of Minturno is considered the ancient Ausonian city, partly because of the polygonal work of the walls. The walls in *opus quadratum* extending out to the western sector, along the Forum, are attributed to the Roman colony of 295 B.C. The principal buildings of the Forum, the Capitolium and portico, are no earlier than the second century. Coins found below the portico date to 200–190 B.C. but the cobblestone canals and a temple identified with the *aedes Iovis* are considered to be earlier. According to Livy, the temple must have been standing in 207 and 191 B.C.[18] He says that it was struck by lightning in those years and destroyed in 191. Architectural terracottas place the origin of the temple at 295 B.C.

A precise chronology of Minturno is lacking, however. The Ostia-type plan of the city may date from the colony of citizens in 295 B.C.; it is similar in size to the colonies at Ostia, Pyrgi, and Pozzuoli. The polygonal work of the walls may date from this time also, although the westward extension of these walls belongs to construction in the following years of the third century.

Pyrgi

Pyrgi, a Roman colony established upon a former Etruscan city, is the third example of a town built on intersecting central axes. The date of its founding is unknown. It is first mentioned in 191 B.C. by Livy (XXXVI, 3, 6). Salmon[19] maintains that the colony was first founded in 194 B.C., a year in which eight maritime colonies were established. Tibiletti[20] thinks, however, that Pyrgi might date from before 194, and now Salmon too proposes a date preceding the first Punic war.[21] Its geographical location and the polygonal work of the walls, comparable to that of Cosa, would suggest a very ancient settlement.

Unfortunately the plan of Pyrgi has been studied little since the early work of Canina and Dennis.[22] An aerial photograph (Fig. 42) permits a simple reconstruction. The area covered by Pyrgi is larger than that of the preceding examples. The city walls, visible throughout, are well preserved, especially on the side of the castle. The southeast wall was short because it is broken by

Figure 42 Pyrgi, aerial view (British School of Rome). British Crown rights reserved.

[18] Livy, XXVII, 37; XXXVI, 37.
[19] *J. Roman Stud.* 26, 1936, p. 51.
[20] *Athenaeum*, N. S., 28, 1950, p. 195, n. 1.
[21] *Phoenix* 9, 1955, p. 66.
[22] G. Dennis, *The Cities and Cemeteries of Etruria*, 2nd ed., London 1883, I, p. 289.

the coastline. Near this break there is a gate, probably open to a road from the center of the city. The missing wall opposite this would also have had a gate. It is possible to reconstruct the axis corresponding to a break in the northeast wall where a gate would have been (Fig. 43).

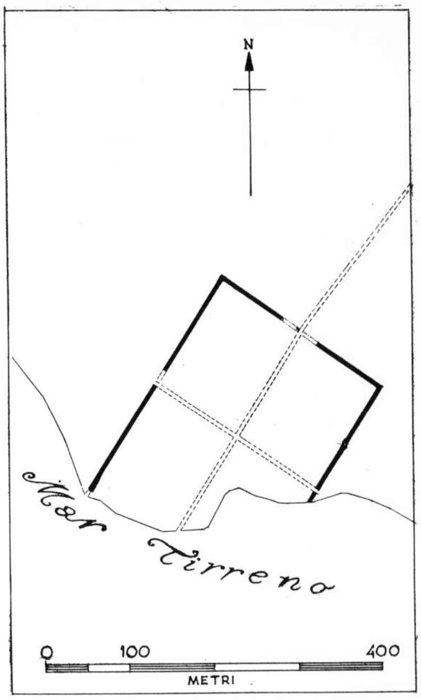

The street pattern of the three cities just described is not known. At Ostia there is a fragment of a street 31 meters southwest of the main *cardine*.

The pattern typical of the Roman city, as we know it from the later examples, is that of a regular network in which a net of streets of equal importance develops parallel to two basic axes that cross usually, but not always, at the center. The network is often enclosed by a square or rectangular perimeter of walls. These cities differ from the Greek and Hellenistic types which have a series of longitudinal axes crossed by narrow transverse streets forming rectangular blocks, and the whole enclosed by an irregular perimeter of walls.

Figure 43 Schematic plan of Pyrgi.

A tentative reconstruction of Terracina,[23] a colony founded in 329 B.C., is possible from a few elements. The Via Appia becomes the *decumanus*, and the principal *cardine* probably ran to the west from the Capitolium, between Porta Nova and the Forum. A pattern of *cardines* 70 meters apart can be deduced from the present layout. It seems as if another *decumanus* ran 50 meters south of the Via Appia. Terracina maintained an irregular perimeter.

Terracina

The walls of Fondi[24] describe an almost square perimeter. Four principal gates correspond to the lines of the major *cardine* and *decumanus*, which are known from the plan that has survived. Minor *cardines* are spaced 50 to 60 meters apart. The location of the lesser *decumani* is uncertain. The polygonal work of the walls may be attributable to the time of the *municipium* with partial rights (338 B.C.), to the time when full rights were granted (188 B.C.),[25] or, as Lugli thinks, about the middle of the third century B.C.[26]

Fondi

Sena Gallica, a colony from 283 B.C., was laid out on a grid of square blocks 50 meters on a side, according to the reconstruction

Senigallia

[23] G. Lugli, *Anxur–Tarracina* (Forma Italiae), Rome 1926.
[24] E. Pais, "Fundi degli Ausoni," in *Studi storici per l'antichità classica*, N.S., I, 1913, p. 30 (see *Dalle guerre puniche a Cesare Augusto*, I, Rome 1918, p. 26). He compares the plan of Fondi with that of the Palatine, seeing a close analogy even in the length of the perimeter walls.
[25] M. E. Blake, *Ancient Roman Construction*, p. 94.
[26] G. Lugli, *La tecnica edilizia in Roma e nel Lazio* (in press).

by Ortolani and Alfieri.[27] This reconstructed plan remains highly hypothetical, however, because it corresponds but little to the existing city.

Rimini

The plan of Ariminum (Rimini), a colony of 268 B.C., is known.[28] It was clearly established on the *cardine* and *decumanus*, each about 9 meters wide, and had blocks 74 by 110 meters (Fig. 44).

Piacenza

Placentia (Piacenza), a colony founded in 218 and reconstructed in 190 B.C., is patterned on a grid of square blocks 80 meters on a side.[29]

Pozzuoli

The blocks at Pozzuoli appear to have similar dimensions. The plan is probably Roman in origin and possibly goes back to the colony of 194, since it is divided into squares. With some 300 colonists, this was a modest town. Though it was neighbor to several Greek cities, Pozzuoli differs substantially from their type of plan. As has been noted, Pozzuoli is usually considered a Greek city, but there are no remains to prove such a time of origin.[30] The Temple of Augustus followed the same orientation.

Bologna

Bologna was established as a colony in 189 B.C.[31] Within its square perimeter, the blocks measure 113,66 by 80 meters. Those adjacent to the *decumanus* are 70 meters wide.

Pesaro

Major axes that meet at the city center remain in Pesaro (184 B.C.). The grid cannot be reconstructed entirely.[32]

Aquileia

Part of the plan of Aquileia (181 B.C.) is known through excavations. A grid, not always uniformly patterned, extended throughout the city. Blocks of 62 by 83 meters have been found.[33]

Parma

The grid pattern of Parma is reflected in the present city and

[27] M. Ortolani and N. Alfieri, "Sena Gallica," *Rend. Lincei* 8, 1953, p. 152. Interamna Lirenas, a colony of 312 B.C., appears to have been laid out on a rectangular grid, although the plan scheme is unknown. Cf. M. Cagiano De Azevedo, *Interamna Lirenas vel Sucasina*, Rome 1947, p. 22.
[28] G. A. Mansuelli, *Ariminum*, Rome 1941; also, *Carta archeologica, Foglio* 101, Florence 1949. Also by the same author, "Additamenta Ariminensia," in *Studi riminesi . . . in onore di C. Lucchesi*, Faenza 1952, p. 113.
[29] M. Corradi-Cervi, E. Nasalli-Rocca, "Placentia," in *Arch. Stor. per le provincie parmensi* III, 1938, p. 57.
[30] *Campanien*, p. 128; Ch. Dubois, "Pouzzoles antique," *Bibl. Ec. Franç.* 98, 1907, p. 231.
[31] P. Ducati, *Storia di Bologna* I, Bologna, 1928, p. 364; E. Andreoli A. Negrioli, *Carta archeologica, foglio* 87, Florence 1938; E. Andreoli, "Bologna nell'antichità," *Mem. Pont. Acc. Arch.* 3, 6, 1943–47, p. 165.
[32] The central axes are: Corso XI Settembre—Via Roma and Via Branca—Via Rossini.
[33] C. Brusin, *Gli scavi di Aquileia*, Udine, 1934.
104

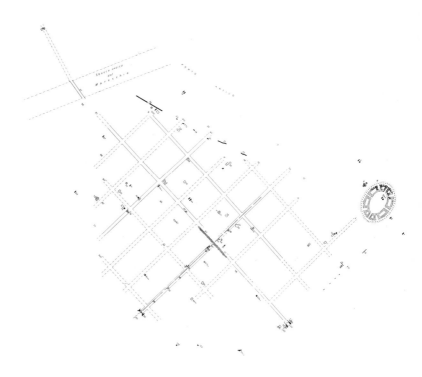

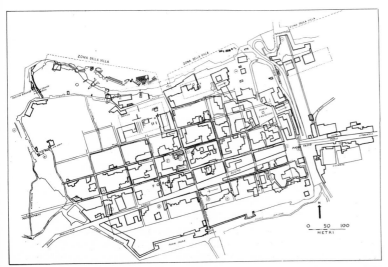

Figure 44 Plan of Rimini (Mansuelli). Scale about 1 : 9000.

Figure 45 Sorrento (Mingazzini–Pfister).

has been confirmed by various findings. The major axes intersect almost at the center, and the blocks are nearly square (45 by 55 meters).[34] It is not known whether this plan corresponds to the original layout of the colony of 183 B.C. or to the rebuilding by Augustus after its destruction in 43 B.C.

Sorrento

Sorrento, reconstructed from the present layout, is thought to be Greek by von Gerkan,[35] for example, and more recently by Mingazzini and Pfister (Fig. 45),[36] who think that the gates and walls are definitely Greek. The disputable point is whether the plan itself should be attributed to the Oscans, Greeks, or the Etruscans, on the basis of research on the unit of measure used for the divisions into blocks (averaging 52 by 76.50 meters).[37] Nonetheless, the town walls—the only elements considered to be of Greek origin—are not placeable at an early date. Rather, according to Lugli,[38] they can be assigned to the era of Silla because of the wide arches. Most probably Sorrento was a colony at that time.

Beloch considered the urban pattern to be of the same type as that of other cities in Campania, except that Sorrento was laid out *per scamna* instead of *per strigas*. (Beloch wrongly supposes this to be true of Pompeii too.) There are other differences, however. Judging by the location of the gates, there is a clear pattern of two central axes. Thus the plan fully agrees with the type of Roman plan we are now discussing, and until contrary proof is offered it must be attributed to the Roman age.

Lucca

Lucca, a colony of 180 or 177 B.C. (although some maintain that it was never granted that status)[39] follows an irregular grid pattern (Fig. 46). The blocks are usually wide, about 75 to 120 meters.[40]

[34] M. Corradi-Cervi, "Nuovi contributi alla topografia di Parma romana imperiale," *Arch. stor. per le provincie parmensi* III, 1938, p. 8, Fig. 2, p. 11.
[35] *Griechische Städteanlagen*, p. 36, p. 92.
[36] P. Mingazzini and F. Pfister, *Surrentum (Forma Italiae)* Florence, 1946, p. 30.
[37] Mingazzini and Pfister, *ibid.*, p. 37. Beloch, *Campanien*, p. 263, lists the short sides as 53–54 meters wide (with the streets, 58–59 meters) and the long sides as 127.5 meters; 75–78 meters; 88 meters; 85 meters; 75 meters; 85 meters; 87 meters. He believes these to have been averaging 200 by 300 feet. A two-acre measure (1 heredium) could be used as a base.
[38] As noted in Mingazzini and Pfister, *Surrentum*, p. 89.
[39] E. T. Salmon, *Class. Quart.* 27, 1933, p. 30; L. Banti, *Mem. Pont. Acc. Arch.* series III, VI, p. 129; A. Bernardi, *Ius Ariminensium, Studia Ghisleriana*, S. I, No. 9, Pavia 1948, p. 247; G. Tibiletti, *Athenaeum* 28, 1950, p. 203.
[40] Marconi takes exception to these measurements, in *Verona romana*, p. 77. Haverfield's reconstruction is incomplete, *Ancient Town-Planning*, p. 96. According to A. Minto, *Not. Scavi* 1925, p. 209, the walls to the north were expanded during a second phase of development. See also D. Albani, *Lucca*, Bologna 1941, p. 7. The street outside the walls to the north is a *cardine* of the centuriation, while the section of the city is bounded by the *decumanus* of the centuriation; see *Stud. Etr.* 20, p. 285.

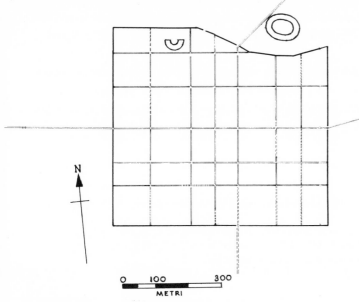

Figure 46 Aerial view and re-constructive scheme of Lucca (British School of Rome). British Crown rights reserved.

N

0 100 300
METRI

107

Florence	The grid of Florentia (Florence) is variously dated between the second century B.C. and the era of the triumvirs. It presents astronomical orientation, a trapezoidal perimeter, an almost central intersection of two major axes, and blocks of varying width, usually square and 60 meters on a side.[41]
Alife	The town of Alife retains a nearly square perimeter of walls (540 by 405 meters) with rounded corners (Fig. 47).[42] The four gates opening near the center of the sides correspond to the major axes which are still part of the present city. A series of secondary streets has also been preserved. These form a network of rect-angles 50 meters wide and of varying lengths. Perhaps the plan belongs to the colony of Silla, which Mommsen believes to have existed,[43] since the walls in *opus incertum* date from that period.[44]
Ascoli	Ascoli Piceno appears to have been divided into square blocks 75 meters on a side. I would say, therefore, that it was probably a Roman city founded after the Social War[45] and not, as Lehmann–Hartleben supposes, a Picene city.[46] He reaches this conclusion on the basis of its relation to the regular plan of Belmonte of the sixth century B.C., which in turn he believes to have been under Etruscan influence.
Como and Pavia	Square blocks from 70 to 80 meters on a side and the central intersection of major axes form the urban pattern of Como[47] (possibly dating from the days of Caesar) and of Pavia[48] (either the first century B.C. or A.D.).
Verona	Verona, built during the first century B.C., perhaps between 75 and 50, is laid out on a uniform grid of almost-square blocks, 75 to 80 meters on a side.[49]
Concordia	Rectangular blocks are found at Concordia, a colony probably founded during the triumvirate.[50]

[41] According to G. Maetzke, *Florentia*, Rome, 1941, p. 28.
[42] D. Marrocco, *L'antica Alife*, Piedimonte d'Alife, 1951.
[43] *Ges. Schriften* V, p. 217.
[44] M. E. Blake, *Ancient Roman Construction*, p. 231.
[45] Walls in *opus incertum* and *opus reticulatum* dated circa 50 B.C.: see also Blake, *ibid.*, p. 233.
[46] Lehmann–Hartleben, *Realencyclopaedie* IIIA, c. 2037.
[47] F. Frigerio, "Comum," in *Lombardia Romana*, Milan, 1938, p. 317.
[48] G. Nocca, "Topografia di Ticinum all'epoca romana," *Atti III Congr. Nazion. Studi Romani*, I, 1934, p. 415; A. Pecora, "Pavia: saggio di geografia urbana," *Rivista geografica italiana*, 61, 1954, p. 281.
[49] P. Marconi, *Verona romana*, Bergamo 1937, p. 77.
[50] P. L. Zovatto, *Antichi monumenti cristiani di Iulia Concordia Sagittaria*, the Vatican, 1950, p. 10, Fig. 1.

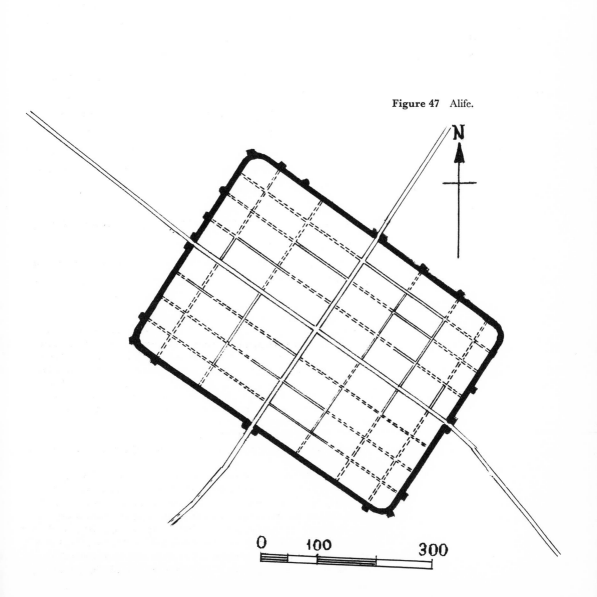

Figure 47 Alife.

Libarna	The grid plan of Libarna[51] dates either from the last days of the Republic or the beginning of the reign of Augustus. Its square blocks are 60 meters on a side.
Augusta Bagiennorum	A grid of varying block size is found at Augusta Bagiennorum.[52] Some of the blocks measure about 80 by 100 meters.
Fano	A square perimeter, a central axis, and a plan oriented to the coastline, apparently with square blocks between 70 and 80 meters wide, characterize the Augustan colony of Fanum Fortunae.
Cities of the Imperial Period	The axial scheme with a grid of square or nearly square blocks was frequently used in the Empire. Among the better-known examples are Emona (34 B.C.), Lincoln, Autun, Trier, Silchester, Caerwent, and Timgad.[53] The blocks are very wide, often more than 100 meters. Timgad is the only exception, with blocks barely 70 feet on a side. An astronomical orientation of the grid was employed frequently.[54]

The Axial Plan as Influenced by the Encampment Plan

Among the varieties of grid plans, a particular Roman type emerges in which the intersection of the major axes is shifted to one side; this is clearly inspired by the military encampments. Instead of the axis conventionally called the *cardine*, there are two parallel axes which we can call the *via principalis* and the *via quintana*, borrowing the terms of the military camps. Turin and Aosta are the best examples.

Turin	The Augustan colony[55] of Turin[56] is a classic example of Roman city planning (Fig. 48) both because of the excellent preservation of the layout in the modern plan and because it was one of the first examples to bring into focus the general problems of delimita-

[51] N. Lamboglia, *Liguria Romana* I, 1939, p. 260.

[52] G. Assandria and G. Vacchetta, *Augusta Bagiennorum*, Benevagienna 1935.

[53] See in particular Lehmann–Hartleben, *Realencyclopaedie*, c. 2087; A. Blanchet, *Les enceintes romaines de la Gaule*, Paris 1907; R. G. Collingwood, *The Archaeology of Roman Britain*, London, 1930, p. 92; W. von Massow, "Zum Stadtbild des spätrömischen Trier, Cardo und Decumanus," *Studies Robinson* I, St. Louis 1951, p. 490. Apparently the plan of Philippopolis (244–249 B.C.) is closer to the Roman plan of *cardine* and *decumanus* than to the Greek type of plan (see von Gerkan, *Griechische Städteanlagen*, p. 136).

[54] See also Barthel, *Bonn. Jahrb.* 120, 1911, p. 99.

[55] Promis (*Storia dell'antica Torino*, Turin, 1869, p. 183) believes the grid to date from the post-Hannibalic period.

[56] Promis, *ibid.* V. Savoja, "Turin, the 'regular' town," *Town Planning Review* 12, 1926–1927, p. 191; G. Bendinelli, *Torino romana*, Turin, 1929; F. Rondolino, "Storia di Torino antica," *Atti Soc. Piemont. di Archeol.* 12, 1930, p. 213; P. Gribaudi, *Lo sviluppo edilizio di Torino dall'epoca romana ai nostri giorni*, Turin 1933 (and *Scritti di varia geografia*, Turin 1955, p. 305); P. Barocelli, *Il Piemonte dalla capanna neolitica ai monumenti di Augusto* III, Turin 1933, p. 47, Fig. 71 (see also, by the same author, *Nuove notizie sulla cinta romana di Torino*, Turin 1936); J. B. Ward Perkins, *Town Planning Review*, 26, 1955, p. 148.

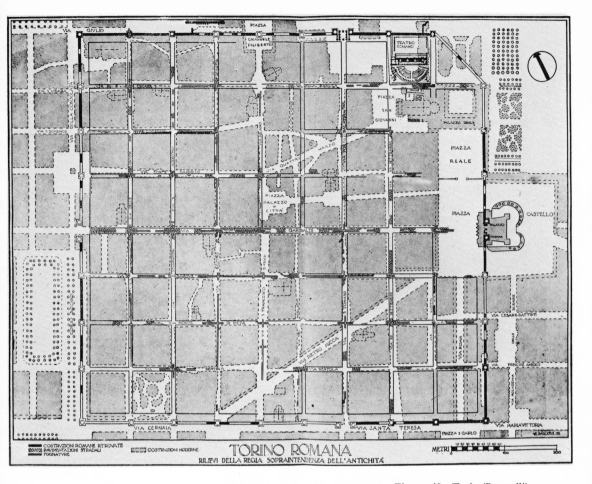

Figure 48 Turin (Barocelli).

111

tion. Turin presents an almost square perimeter[57] which appears to have been 669 by 720 meters or 20 actus.[58] A grid of streets 5 to 8 meters wide[59] defines blocks some 2 actus to a side. There are 7 streets in one direction, 8 in the other. The intersection of the major axes does not occur at the center. In fact, although the northwest-to-southeast axis (Corso Garibaldi) is in the center, the axis orthogonal to this that leads to the Porta Palatina is far to the eastern side of the city (Via dell'Arsenale—San Tommaso —Porta Palatina). This corresponds to the *via principalis* of the camps. It is not by chance that one of the parallel streets in the eastern sector was called *via quintana*.

Aosta

Aosta's plan is very similar to that of Turin (Fig. 49). Its walls form a rectangle 724 by 572 meters. Apparently the intention was to establish a rectangle of 20 actus by 16. The 6 or 7 meters on each side which were in excess of this measure perhaps represent the thickness of the walls or of the *pomerium*. The pattern of the sewage system indicates a grid of seven *cardines* and seven *decumani*,[60] subdividing blocks of about 70 to 80 meters on a side, as at Turin. Furthermore, two of the *cardines* appear particularly important in that they lead to the city gates. We can call them *via principalis* and *via quintana*, and in fact medieval documents of Aosta also refer to a street called *via quintana*.[61]

Axial Plan with Subdivision *per scamna*

Among the plans characterized by a network of square or nearly square blocks, a type can be distinguished in which the central division by main *decumanus* and *cardine* is accompanied by blocks whose long side runs parallel to the *decumanus*. These blocks are termed *scamna*.

Carthage

Roman Carthage is the best example of this type of plan (Fig. 50). Its layout has been reconstructed by C. Saumagne and P. Davin[62] from the ruins of the sewer system (besides several monuments such as the cisterns of Bordj Djedid which occupy an entire block). They were able to reconstruct a rigorous uniform grid of streets which delineate very long rectangular blocks. Calculations show the roads to have been 24 feet (7.06 meters)

[57] Unless the east corner is modified.
[58] According to Rondolino the sides measure 702 by 760 meters.
[59] Known to exist from various excavations and findings.
[60] See P. Barocelli, *Augusta Praetoria (Forma Italiae)* Rome, 1948, c. 74; J. B. Ward Perkins, *Town Planning Review* 26, 1955, Plates XXII and XXIII.
[61] C. Promis, *Le antichità di Aosta*, Turin, 1862, p. 139. Nicopolis in Mesia, founded by Trajan, is a similar example; see G. Kazarow, Pauly–Wissowa, *Realencyclopaedie* 17, 1936, c. 527.
[62] C. Saumagne, "Colonia Iulia Karthago," *Bull. Arch. Comité* 1924, p. 131; P. Davin, "Etude sur la cadastration de la Colonia Iulia Carthago," *Revue Tunisienne* N.S., I, 1930, p. 73.

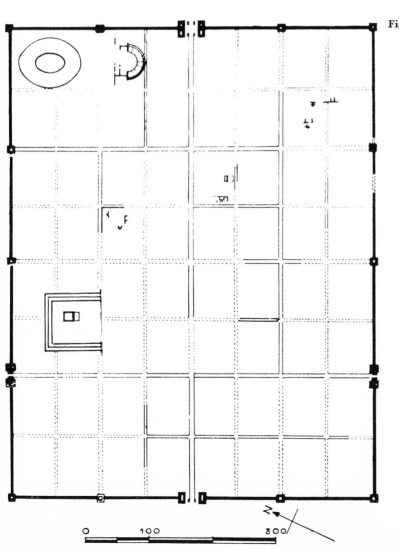

Figure 49 Aosta

0   100   300

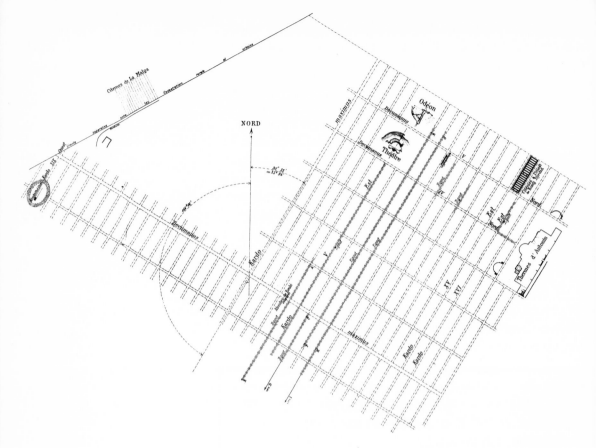

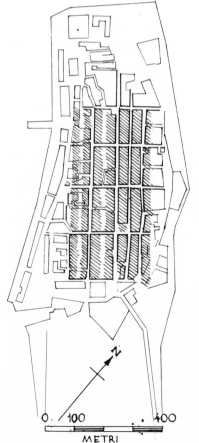

Figure 50 Carthage (Davin).

Figure 51 Zara.

wide, except for the major axes which were 40 feet (11.76 meters) wide. The blocks measure 35.28 by 141.12 meters (1 by 4 actus). Thus the area enclosed is 2 square actus or 2 jugers or 1 heredium. The rectangular blocks should be considered *scamna* rather than *strigae* because the road that has been termed the *cardine maximus* was more likely the *decumanus maximus*, being parallel to the coast line.

That the city is Roman and not Punic is attested by the numerous Punic tombs, dating at least from the third century B.C.[63] Whether this Carthage was the colony of Gracchus from 122 B.C. or belonged to the Augustan era, 35–15 B.C. remains to be decided. The latter date is generally accepted because the grid layout of the city appears to derive from the land assignment and survey of 122 B.C.

The same general scheme and dimensions found at Carthage were very likely employed in the Augustan colony of Zara (Iader) (Fig. 51); the *scamna* measure 1 by 4 actus (an area of 2 jugers). The use of subdivision by rectangles continues into the Imperial period. It is found in the Severian city of Leptis,[64] where the blocks are unusually small, and at Sufetula,[65] where the blocks measure 50 by 100 meters.

Zara

The Hippodamean plan has inspired not only the cities here discussed but also the form of the Roman military encampment. As already noted, especially in regard to the plan of Ostia, the encampment does not entirely follow the so-called *castrum* scheme with its central intersection of the major axes. Instead, as found in Polybius (VI, 26–42) and throughout much archeological documentation, the encampment is patterned along the *via principalis* (100 feet wide according to Polybius 28, 1) and the *via quintana*. The blocks, whose long dimension is at right angles to the major roads, are subdivided by secondary streets. So arrayed, they are termed *strigae* by Iginus Gromaticus (*De munit. castrorum* 1). Rectangles arranged parallel to the major axes are termed *scamna*.

Encampment Plan

Streets perpendicular to the *via principalis* and *via quintana* are of lesser importance. Aside from a basic Hippodamean layout, the plans show a tendency toward centralization in that there is a gate at the center of each short side and that the perimeter walls

---

[63] G. Pinza, *Mem. Lincei* 30, 1925, c. 53; B. Pace, *ibid.*, c. 141.
[64] J. B. Ward Perkins, *J. Rom. Stud.* 38, 1948, p. 59.
[65] A. Merlin, *Forum et églises de Sufetula, Notes et documents publiés par la Direction des Antiquités de la Tunisie*, V, 1912, Plate 1.

are square or almost square. Other than the reports of Polybius, Schulten's work has been chiefly responsible for bringing to light a series of Republican encampments near Numantia (see Figs. 52 to 54 for the camp of the consul Fulvius Nobilior of 153 B.C., the camp of Marcellus at Castillejo in 151 B.C., and camp V in the same zone, later than 90 B.C.[66]).

The same scheme is found during the Imperial era, at Carnuntum (Fig. 55) and at Lambesi, for example. Also at the Castra Praetoria of Rome, dwelling units arranged *per strigas* have been found, each half an actus wide.[67] The direction of these *strigae* is a decisive element in determining the principal axis and thus the orientation of the Castra Praetoria (Fig. 56). Then the *porta principalis sinistra* would face toward Rome.[68]

Another type of encampment is based on the central intersection of a *cardine* and *decumanus*, as at Ostia and other cities. Examples of this type are found in England, Germany, and Syria.[69]

Yet the basic plan remains similar to the type assigned to Hippodamus of Miletus. With this in mind, Polybius's comparison between encampment and city can be better understood (VI, 31, 10):

τὸ μὲν σύμπαν σχῆμα γίνεται τῆς στρατοπεδείας τετράγωνον ἰσόπλευρον, τὰ δὲ κατὰ μέρος ἤδη τῆς τε ῥυμοτομίας ἐν αὐτῇ καὶ τῆς ἄλλης οἰκονομίας πόλει παραπλησίαν ἔχει τὴν διάθεσιν. (The whole camp forms a square, and the way in which the streets are laid out and its general arrangement give it the appearance of a town.) Here Polybius is not drawing a parallel between the square *castrum* and the *urbs quadrata* such as Ostia, as a hasty reading would suggest; only in the second part of the passage does he make a comparison between the *castrum* and the city (τὰ δὲ . . .), that is the ῥυμοτομία and the οἰκονομία noted by von Gerkan.[70] The comparison between Republican encampment and Hippodamean city is quite exact, especially because the subdivision *per strigas* and the pattern of two major east–west axes were employed in both.

---

[66] A. Schulten, *Numantia*, III and IV, Munich 1929.
[67] Cf. Hygin, *De mun. castr.* 1: *efficitur striga pedum sexaginta*.
[68] The orientation (mistaken in the *Forma* of Lanciani) was correctly derived from the location of the gates by U. Antonielli, "Sull'orientamento dei Castra Pretoria," *Bull. Com.* 41, 1913, p. 31. See further G. Zanghieri, "Castro Pretorio," *Boll. dell'Istituto storico e di cultura dell'arma del Genio*, 1948, p. 30. The encampment measures 1300 by 1500 feet (380 by 440 meters).
[69] For example, see R. G. Collingwood, *The Archaeology of Roman Britain*, London, 1930, p. 14; *Der obergermanisch-raetische Limes*, Berlin–Leipzig, 1936 and following; A. Poidebard, *La trace de Rome dans le desert de Syrie*, Paris 1934.
[70] *Griechische Städteanlagen*, p. 90.

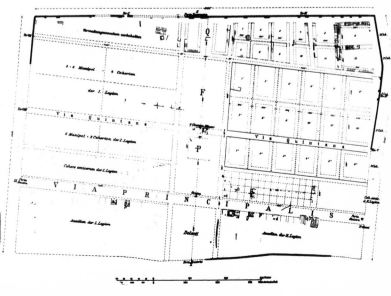

Figure 52 Camp of Nobilior.

Figure 53 Camp V of Castillejo near Numantia (Schulten).

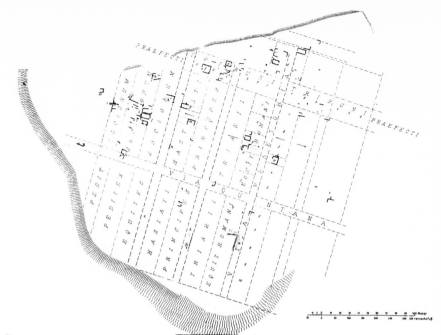

Figure 54   Camp of Marcellus near Numantia (Schulten).

Figure 55   Carnuntum, camp (*Der röm. Limes in Österreich*).

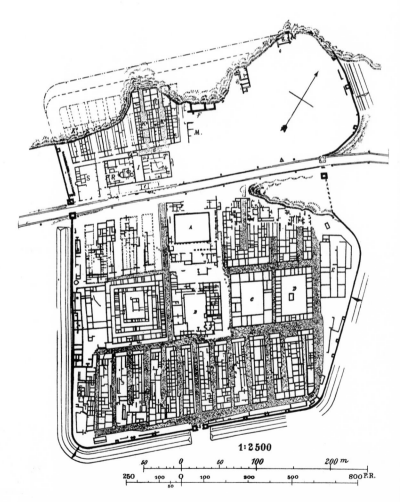

118

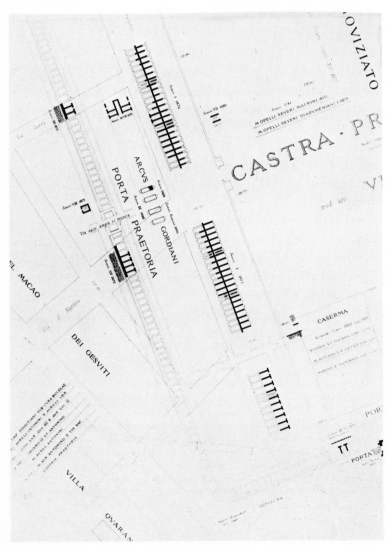

Figure 56 Castra Praetoria, showing the *strigae* (Lanciani).

According to Frontinus[71] the Romans did not use encampments before the time of Pyrrhus. This would seem to rule out the consideration of Ostia, which is older than that, as an encampment plan. However, as was observed earlier in this chapter, the two types of plans are independent. In considering whether the city derived from the military camp, or vice versa, the answer is that the encampment's form seems to have come from the Hippodamean city.

Characteristics of the Uniform Roman City

The uniform Roman city as known from the fourth century onward has assumed a large variety of forms when compared to the Greek city type. These forms are:
1. The city derived from the Hippodamean type, subdivided *per strigas* (except Alba, which is patterned on *scamna*).
2. The central crossing of axes scheme, with a system of parallel streets almost always forming a square or nearly-square grid.
3. A variation of 2, based on the layout of military encampments.
4. A system of central axes with subdivision *per scamna*.

These variations paralleled the different agrarian subdivisions. The first system is directly comparable to the agrarian division *per strigas*; the second is like the traditional centuriation. The fourth scheme corresponds to the *ager per centurias et scamna adsignatus*. It should be noted that the various systems of land division can be traced back just as far as the systems for patterning cities (the centuriation of Terracina in 329, the *strigatio* of Suessa Aurunca in 313 B.C.).

There is no overlap among the various city systems. Cosa, belonging to type 1, comes close to being of the fourth type because some of its axes appear to be more important than others. Among the cities having a central intersection of axes there is a wide variety in the proportions of the blocks. In fact there is so much variety that cities such as Sorrento and especially Alife are considered to be close to the fourth type.

---

[71] Frontinus, *Strateg.* IV, 1, 14: *Castra antiquitus Romani ceteraeque gentes passim per corpora cohortium velut mapalia constituere soliti erant, cum solos urbium muros nosset antiquitas. Pyrrhus Epirotarum rex primus totum exercitum sub eodem vallo continere instituit. Romani deinde, victo eo in campis Arusinis circa urbem Malventum, castris eius potiti et ordinatione notata paulatim ad hanc usque metationem, quae nunc effecta est, pervenerunt.* (In ancient times the Romans and other peoples used to make their camps like groups of Punic huts, distributing the troops here and there by cohorts, since the men of old were not acquainted with walls except in the case of cities. Pyrrhus, king of the Epirotes, was the first to inaugurate the custom of concentrating an entire army within the precincts of the same entrenchments. Later the Romans, after defeating Pyrrhus on the Arusian Plains near the city of Maleventum, captured his camp, and, noting its plan, gradually came to the arrangement which is in vogue today.)

A wide variety is found also in the dimensions of the city blocks. Hippodamean cities usually have blocks 1 actus wide and usually more than twice as long. In the plans with almost square blocks the most common dimensions are between 70 and 80 meters. An area of two jugers seems to have been preferred.

At times the grid followed a celestial orientation (in Florence and perhaps Lucca) but more often conditions were set by geographical configurations such as coast lines (Pyrgi, Carthage, Fano, Pesaro), rivers (Ostia, Minturno), major communications arteries (Terracina, Fondi), or mountains (Norba, Alba, Cosa). The Forum is normally found at the intersection of the major axes.

The chief interest in these regular Roman cities lies naturally in those types, such as Ostia, which were inspired by the principle of axial symmetry, developed without imitation of the encampments. As has been said earlier, this principle is not typical of Italy, and its origins are traceable to the Greeks rather than to the Etruscans and Italics. However, it was in Roman colonies from the fourth century on that axial symmetry found its most rigorous application, extending even to the perimeter of the quadrangular or square city, and it was here that it was most extensively used. Such a rich production of cities and widespread use of agrarian surveying was quite naturally the object of much theorizing by scholars of the late Republic. Yet the Roman urban planner was little moved by celestial speculation and adopted the principles of axial symmetry because they corresponded to Roman taste. For example, this symmetry appears in the atrium-type house as well as in the Imperial Forum. Furthermore, axial symmetry embodied the concept of military discipline and centralized political power, focusing the city upon a single point,[72] where the magistrate exercised his authority. The same was true of the military camp. This idea of a central focus becomes more evident when the Roman plan is contrasted to the layout of the Hippodamean city, in which the uniformity of the pattern is accompanied by the concept of decentralization. This is characteristic of the Greek city, because it corresponds to the looser political plan.[73]

[72] As von Gerkan would have us believe, *Griechische Städteanlagen*, p. 128.
[73] See the observations made by Tritsch, "Die Stadtbildungen des Altertums und die griechische Polis," *Klio*, 22, 1928, pp. 1–83.

Conclusion

The irregular pattern of Rome, clearly resulting from the lack of a master plan, is defined by Livy (V, 55, 5): *forma . . . urbis . . . occupatae magis quam divisae similis.* The regularity or irregularity of town forms depends entirely on the presence or absence of spontaneity in their birth and growth. The irregular city is the result of development left entirely to individuals who actually live on the land. If a governing body divides the land and disposes of it before it is handed over to the users, a uniformly patterned city will emerge. In accordance with this rather obvious determinant, Athens and Rome had to be irregular in pattern. The regular plan is found in Greek and Roman colonies and in cities that had been subjected to complete destruction and rebuilding. Most especially, uniformity is found in colonies where egalitarianism prevailed. Compare Roman and Greek colonies with those of the seventeenth and eighteenth centuries, formed on a rigid chessboard plan: Buenos Aires, Lima, Philadelphia, and so on.

Regular planning took form in the ancient cities chiefly by use of orthogonal subdivisions, as it did also in the colonial cities just mentioned and in certain medieval cities.[1] It can also be seen in entirely different environments, among the Aztecs and at Peking even at the time of Marco Polo. More than from ritual values, the orthogonal system was employed because of its practicality and aesthetic appeal.[2] There are no records in the ancient world of other regular forms such as the circular, star-shaped, and polygonal plans known in the Renaissance and Baroque eras, inspired by theories of the ideal city or of scenographic effects.

The orthogonal plan mirrors a principle widely known throughout the Orient and among the Minoans–Mycenaeans; the plan is so basic in nature that we need not look for any derivation. There seem to be no pathways for adopting Oriental styles, with the exception of some Egyptian influence. Diffusion of the orthogonal style cannot be attributed to the Phoenecians, for Soluntum and Selinus are Greek cities, not Punic.

The orthogonal system arose first from the right-angle intersection of two roads; it is found in the sixth-century Greek world no less than in the Etrusco–Italian settlements. Orthogonal plans are therefore not to be considered specific to Etrusco–Italian ur-

---

[1] See S. Lang, "Sull'origine della disposizione a scacchiera nelle città medievali in Inghilterra, Francia e Germania," *Palladio* N.S., 5, 1955, p. 97.
[2] P. Lavedan, *Qu'est-ce que l'Urbanisme?*, Paris 1926, p. 63; also F. Paulsen, "Der rechte Winkel im Städtebau," *Monatsh. f. Baukunst u. Städtebau* 1933, p. 233.

124

banism. The importance of this type of urbanism must be sharply limited when we exclude not only the terremare settlements but also Marzabotto, Capua, and Roma Quadrata and when we attribute the theories of the *gromatici* to the erudition of the late Republic.

On the other hand, the division by means of *strigae*, usually one actus wide, is interesting. It is documented in both the Greek and Etruscan cultures from the first half of the fifth century and must be allied to the work of Hippodamus of Miletus. This common urban style, expressed in both design and measurement, is one of the clearest expressions of the ties between Greece and Italy.

Although the Hippodamean plan is employed through the Hellenistic era, it is used in only a few cities by the Romans because in the fourth century B.C. the centralized plan began to be developed. Compared with the monotonous repetition of the plan as used in the Hellenistic world, the Romans achieved considerable variety in type of design and range of dimensions.

Uniform planning as developed in the ancient world included the theoretical study of climate and sociology. Theory preceded the practice of the planners and followed it as well. The studies that followed their work not only adhered to reality, as in Hippocrates, Aristotle, and Vitruvius, but also ventured into fantasy, creating ideal cities, as we see in Plato and Aristophanes, or refinements rooted in cosmic concepts, as in the Roman doctrine of delimitation.

Appendix (1970)

The original text of 1956 (Rome, De Luca publishers) is un-
changed in this book, except that translations of Latin and Greek
passages have been added. The same illustrations are used
throughout. Yet it is important to add to this text information
on discoveries and discussions that have taken place since the
original publication. We will refer exclusively to those studies
that most impinge upon Hippodamean urbanism, and it is in
this context that we have chosen to review the vast and often
overlapping bibliography.[1]

Our knowledge of ancient city planning has greatly increased,
largely because of recent excavations and aerial surveys. The
acceptance and widespread use of the rectangular plan, particularly in the cities of Magna Graecia and Sicily, is more apparent than ever. Because of the excavations of Metaponto and
the studies carried out at Selinus, we must extend our chronology
to include the second half of the sixth century B.C.[2] These older
limiting dates again bring up the question whether it is legitimate
to use the term Hippodamean to qualify these examples of
urbanism. Certainly we must exclude from our discussion those

[1] Among the general discussions of rectangular city planning in the classical
world, we must single out (aside from those studies concerning specific cities)
the following important works: A. Kriesis, "Ancient Greek Town Building,"
Acta Congressus Madvigiani 4, Copenhagen, 1958, p. 27 (republished with several
other studies in the volume by the same author, in *Greek Town Building*,
Athens, 1965); A. Boethius, "Problemi connessi con l'architettura romana,"
Palladio 8, 1958, p. 1; also *The Golden House of Nero*, Ann Arbor, Mich., 1960,
p. 26 and "Urbanistica," *Enciclopedia Arte Antica*, 1966, vol. 7, p. 1067; J. Ward
Perkins, "The Early Development of Roman Town Planning," *Acta Congressus
Madvigiani* 4, Copenhagen, 1958, p. 109; H. Rosenau, *The Ideal City*, London,
1959; E. Kirsten, "Die Entstehung der griechischen Stadt," *Arch. Anz.* 1964,
c. 892. Broad discussions are to be found in the general treatises on Greek
town planning, especially those of R. Martin, *L'urbanisme dans la Grèce antique*,
Paris, 1956 (see also the review by A. Kriesis in *Gnomon* 29, 1957, p. 359) and
those by A. Giuliano, *La città greca*, Rome, 1961, and *Urbanistica delle città
greche*, Milan, 1966; A. Garcia y Bellido, *Urbanistica de las grandes ciudades del
mundo antiguo*, Madrid 1966. See also M. Coppa, *Storia dell'urbanistica dalle
origini all'ellenismo*, Turin, 1968; G. Schmiedt, *Atlante delle sedi umane in Italia*, II,
Florence, 1970; G. A. Mansuelli, *Architettura e città*, Bologna 1970. F. Castag-
noli, "La pianta di Metaponto: Ancora sull'urbanistica ippodamea," *Rend.
Lincei* 14, 1959, p. 49; "Recenti ricerche sull'urbanistica ippodamea," *Arch.
Class.* 15, 1963, p. 180; and "Note di architettura e di urbanistica," *Arch.
Class.* 20, 1968, p. 117, and finally some articles in *Studi sulla città antica*,
Bologna 1970.
It is important also to note the interesting discussions of the organizational
structure of the Greek city and its limits related to the human dimension, by
C. A. Doxiadis in "The Ancient Greek City and the City of the Present,"
The Living Heritage of Greek Antiquity, Paris, 1967, p. 192.
[2] An earlier date, corresponding to the founding of the city, is proposed for
Metaponto, and possibly for Paestum, Selinus, and Agrigento, by A. Giuliano,
Urbanistica. This hypothesis is further discussed by A. Di Vita, "Per l'architettura
e l'urbanistica greca d'età arcaica: La stoa nel temenos del tempio C e lo
sviluppo programmato di Selinunte," *Palladio* 7, 1967, p. 46. For a similar
dating of Paestum, see also G. Voza, *Arch. Class.* 15, 1963, p. 232; Coppa,
Storia dell'urbanistica; and M. T. Manni Peraino, *Parola del Passato*, 23, 1968,
p. 430.

hypotheses which attribute to Hippodamus the radial plan or the monumental (scenographic) city plan.[3] The first problem is a historiographic one—to decide what Aristotle meant by διαίρεσις τῶν πόλεων. Evidently he was alluding to the widespread rectangular city plan which we know to be associated with his century and those immediately preceding it—a plan which, with some important variations, had close structural relations throughout the Greek world.

The next question is to establish the correct reference of the Aristotelian statement. Examples of Hippodamean cities like Metaponto, that certainly preceded Hippodamus, lead us to conclude with even more assurance that Hippodamus was not the creator of this type of city planning; his name is linked with it only through his studies of the political organization and the social system, and especially through his planning of Piraeus.

Hippodamean city planning is a unique chapter in the history of urban planning not only for the concept of a master plan to control all future growth and development,[4] but also for its rational organic qualities. To recapitulate, these are summarized as follows: The street grid is regularly subdivided into wide parallel strips by a very few (usually only three or four) major longitudinal arteries. At right angles to these run other streets, a few of which are major communication roads but most of which are narrow alleyways whose only purpose is to create blocks for buildings. The blocks thus formed are usually long and narrow. Buildings and plazas fall within the grid. There is no central intersection of major axes (as distinguished from the Roman axial grid). Throughout, the grid is derived from certain fixed dimensions (the short side of the block in particular was often set at 120 feet). Aside from a strictly rational and geometric form, the grid exemplified certain criteria of absolute equality among the residential blocks. If this spirit of equality was previously thought to be in keeping with the constitutional democracies of the fifth century B.C., we must now observe that by placing the more ancient plans in the sixth century we find an entirely different social system—that is, strong tyrannical governments capable of exercising total and complete planning authority. We must also keep in mind, of course, the often noted connection with colonialism.

[3] Giuliano, *Urbanistica* (especially p. 105) denies the relationship of the sixth-century colonial cities with the Hippodamean city of the fifth century B.C.
[4] The same general intent has been observed in the plan of Megara Hyblea, in the second half of the seventh century B.C. (G. Vallet and F. Villard, *Mél. Ec. Franç.* 81, 1969, p. 7). This plan is very important, particularly because it lacks the rectangular grid, thus differing from the other plans considered here.

It must be added that these conclusions may be modified by subsequent discoveries. For example, many elements basic to Hippodamean planning are to be found at the acropolis of Zernaki Tepe in Urartu, although organized on an axial scheme. If this plan can be decisively dated in the eighth century B.C., we are forced to conclude that the Hippodamean plan of the sixth century was not a spontaneous creation but rather a gradual evolution of an archaic Anatolian tradition, possibly by way of the Ionian world.

Another important point of discussion, the relation of the Hippodamean plan to the Italic and Etruscan cultures, has not been modified by new material and discoveries. Two fundamental points still hold: the theory of the celestial *templum* has no relation whatsoever to city planning; and Marzabotto is a Greek plan. Because of the limited evidence, we must still consider these to be provisional conclusions; nevertheless the Etruscans cannot be thought of as having played a completely autonomous role in the use and development of Hippodamean urbanism, nor is there evidence of the sacred nature of the Hippodamean city plan. There is even less reason to suppose a relation between the uniform grid plan of the Etruscan cities and either certain prehistoric antecedents or *Roma quadrata*.

It should not be necessary to repeat that the monotonous regularity of these plans does not mean that Hippodamean cities were esthetically unpleasing. The third dimension, the elevation is often missing; yet without doubt the differing volumes of the buildings and architectonic variation offered by the porticoes, public buildings and imposing temples would ensure a freedom of architectural solutions despite the restrictions of the plan. Often, as at Paestum and Agrigento, the temples were oriented independently of the grid, for religious reasons. Certainly the uniformity and repetitiveness of the basic grid did not prevent the planners from exploiting the natural terrain, as at Rhodes, Priene, and Soluntum.

There follows from this general discussion a series of notes and observations on problems considered in the body of the book.

p. 10. Cities of the sixth and fifth centuries, B.C.

The plan of the acropolis of Selinus must be classified separately from those of the rectangular axial intersection type. Excavations in the last few years have shown that the plan is not derived from an axial intersection to which the grid of the blocks was added during the fourth century, but rather from a plan developed at one time. It is best interpreted as comprising two

130

east–west πλατεῖαι and one running north–south. The short sides
of the blocks were established on the former, and the blocks
were divided north–south by narrow στενωποί. Only in the
northern sector were the στενωποί laid out east–west because of
the narrowing of the hill and the obvious space restrictions
resulting. Selinus therefore is of the Hippodamean *per strigas* type,
laid out in accordance with the topographic limitations.[5] The
plan should be placed toward the second half of the sixth century.[6]

The archaic streets would appear to coincide with the grid system
developed during the fifth century B.C.[7]

p. 12. Miletus

The rectangular layout of Rhodes was also observed by J. Bradford, working from an aerial survey,[8] at the same time as J.
Kondis observed it, but independently. The latter, in a new
study of the plan,[9] maintains that the city was built up by small
blocks 100 by 150 feet, ascertained principally by the remaining
streets and discovery of ancient elements, mainly sewers. But it
seems possible that certain of the sewers belong to the internal
ambitus of the blocks. I have therefore put forward the hypothesis
that Rhodes should be reconsidered on the basis of larger blocks,
with the long axis running north–south.[10] From excavations in
recent years we can deduce that this was indeed the direction
of the long axis of the blocks; as for the dimensions, the short
side of the blocks has now been confirmed at about 49 meters.[11]

p. 14. Rhodes

In the documentation of this plan by Diodorus (XII, 10, 7)
Kondis[12] interprets the much disputed passage (τῶν ὑπὸ δὲ τούτων

p. 18. Thurii

[5] See F. Castagnoli, *Arch. Class.* 15, 1963, p. 184; A. Di Vita "Per l'architettura,"
p. 41. According to Kriesis, *Greek Town Building*, p. 69, we have instead an
axial plan probably of Etruscan influence. According to Martin, *L'urbanisme*,
p. 89, the uniformity of the plan is only apparent, being actually the product
of a slow evolution.
[6] I. Bovio Marconi, "Scavi a Selinunte," in *Urbanistica* March 1958, p. 76.
Also see *VII Cong. Intern. Arch. Class.* II, Rome 1961, p. 11, A. Di Vita, in
"Per l'architettura." For a discussion of Olbia, see also C. M. Danoff, in
Pauly–Wissowa *Realencyclopaedie*, suppl. 8, 1962, c. 1092.
[7] *Amer. Journ. Arch.* 65, 1961, p. 47; and 67, 1963, p. 185.
[8] J. Bradford, *Ancient Landscapes*, London 1956, p. 277 (with bibliography).
[9] J. Kondis, "Zum antiken Stadtbauplan von Rhodos," *Athen. Mitt.* 73, 1958,
p. 146. Of particular interest are Kondis's findings in regard to the width of some of
the πλατεῖαι, as much as 9.30 and 16.10 meters, and the continuity of the grid
even in the hilly region.
[10] See F. Castagnoli, *Arch. Class.* 15, 1963, p. 183. For Rhodes and Hippodamus
see also n. 33, p. 135.
[11] Gr. Konstantinopoulos, Ἀρχ. Δελτ. 22, 1967, part 2 (published 1969), p. 514.
[12] I. D. Kondis, Ἡ διαίρεσις τῶν Θουρίων in Ἀρχ. Ἐφημ., 1956 (published 1959),
p. 106, 216. For an interpretation of the plan layout of Thurii, see also C. H.
Kraeling, *Ptolemais*, Chicago, 1962, p. 48. Also an excellent aerial photograph
of Euesperides has been published by R. C. Bond and J. M. Swales, *Lybia
Antiqua* II, 1965, Table 39.

στενωπῶν πεπληρωμένων τὰς οἰκίας ἡ πόλις ἐφαίνετο καλῶς πεπλερωμένων) in a new way. He nonetheless arrives at the usual interpretation concerning the counterposition between πλατεῖαι and στενωποί and in attributing to Thurii a plan analogous to that of Rhodes.

p. 19. Agrigento

The Olympieion (480–460 B.C.) has been to date the *ante quem* reference for the entire plan of Agrigentum, yet recent stratigraphic excavations in the Hellenistic quarters have revealed structures datable to the second half of the sixth century.[13]

pp. 24, 35

We must take note of discussions concerning the plans of Naples and of Pompeii and of their chronology.[14]

p. 39. Paestum

The plan layout of the city[15] must be placed at an earlier date. A more ancient *terminus ante quem* than those so far considered is found in the subterranean temple[16] datable shortly after 510 B.C. Recent exploratory excavations within the residential sectors indicate a similar period.

Paestum is to be considered a clear example of Hippodamean urbanism as characterized by the elongated proportions of the blocks and notable absence of an axial intersection. Yet there has been no lack of opposing evaluations: thus von Gerkan[17] transposes the dates into the Lucanian era, and Schläger reaches similar conclusions.[18] Paestum, based on a strong axial scheme, is thus typically Italic according to von Gerkan.

[13] See E. De Miro, "Il quartiere ellenistico romano di Agrigento " *Mem. Linc.* 8, 12, 1957, p. 138. See also R. Martin, *L'urbanism*, p. 89. The aerial photographs which revealed the plan of Agrigento have been republished with a new interpretation by G. Schmiedt and P. Griffo, "Agrigento antica dalle fotografie aeree e dai recenti scavi," *Universo*, 1958, p. 289.
[14] For Pompeii, see P. Ciprotti, *Studia et documenta historiae et iuris* 23, 1957, p. 331, and M. Napoli, *Napoli Greco-romana*, Naples, 1959, p. 89. O. Elie, in *Studi sulla città antica*, Bologna 1970, p. 183; H. Eschebach, *Die Städtebauliche Entwicklung des antiken Pompeji* (Röm. Mitt., 17. E.), 1970. For Naples, see M. Napoli, *op. cit.*, p. 75, 80; C. Di Seta, *Cartografia della città di Napoli*, Naples, 1959, p. 96; W. Johannowsky, *Boll. d'Arte* 45, 1960, p. 210; G. Russo, *Edilizia a Napoli dalle origini sino al 1870*, Naples, 1961; F. Castagnoli, *Arch. Class.* 15, 1963, p. 186; P. G. Hamberg, "Vitruvius, Fra Giocondo and the City Plan of Naples," in *Acta Arch.* 36, 1965, p. 105 (interesting in particular for the terminology relating to the streets and for a study of the Vitruvian urbanistic practices of the Renaissance); W. Döpp, *Die Altstadt Neapels, Entwicklung und Struktur*, Marburg, 1968.
[15] To consult the aerial photographs from which the city plan was reconstructed, see also J. Bradford, *Ancient Landscapes*, London, 1957, p. 218, Fig. 52; W. Müller, "Der wiedergefundene Plan der Städte der antiken Welt in der aerofotografischen Dokumentation," *Wiss. Zeitschr. d. Hochschule f. Architektur u. Bauwesen*, Weimar 9, 1962, H. 3.
[16] See also F. Castagnoli, *Arch. Class.* 15, 1963, p. 188.
[17] A. von Gerkan, "Zur Stadtlage von Paestum," in *Studii Calderini Paribeni* 3, Milano 1956, p. 211. See also A. Boethius, *Golden House*, p. 36, n. 13; M. W. Frederiksen, *Gnomon* 34, 1962, p. 296.
[18] H. Schläger, *Röm. Mitt.* 72, 1962, p. 188. See also F. Castagnoli, *Arch. Class.* 15, 1963, p. 187 (concerning also the hypothesis of a road between Porta

The methodical excavations that have been undertaken enrich our understanding of this plan, important to the study of ancient urbanism.[19] The most notable of the recent finds are the discovery that the sacred buildings (acropolis) are perfectly aligned with the urban grid pattern, and the finding of a stone plate under the road surface at the intersection of two πλατεῖαι on which were incised two orthogonal lines. Although other such plates, without incisions, have been found at other intersections, it is improbable that they were part of a sacred ritual belonging to the celestial *templum* of the *Etrusca disciplina*. In all probability they were part of the normal technical operations performed during the layout of the streets. I therefore maintain that Marzabotto is to be placed among the examples of Greek urban design.

Additional examples of Hippodamean cities of the sixth and fifth centuries can now be cited.

The vast city of Metaponto[20] is built with a rectangular layout based on a few πλατεῖαι intersected perpendicularly by two πλατεῖαι and numerous στενωποί, The blocks measure one actus by one stadius (as at Naples). The temple of Apollo Lykeios serves as an *ante quem* reference, insofar as its congruity with the grid pattern presupposes at least the prior existence of the street grid. The present temple is datable toward the beginning of the fifth century, but recently a more ancient lower temple has been discovered.

The subdivision *per strigas* with elongated blocks (whose short sides are 34.25, 34.40, and 34.90 meters, and long sides about 78 meters, although the intersections are not perfectly orthogonal)

Aurea and Porta Giustizia, parallel to the temples and in existence prior to the urban grid); *ibid.* 20, 1968, p. 122. For the passage from Strabo, see M. Mello, "Strabone V, 14, 13 e le origini di Poseidone," *Parola del Passato* 22, 1967, p. 401.

[19] See G. A. Mansuelli, *Arte antica e moderna* 17, 1962, p. 14, *Röm. Mitt.* 70, 1963, p. 44; *Parola del Passato* 20, 1965, p. 314, 325; *Studi storichi* 8, 1967, p. 5. See also F. Castagnoli, *Arcd. Class.* 20, 1968, p. 119. For the stones found at street intersections, comparison should be made with the pillar found at Cividale (Forum Iulii) incised with axial lines, which was recovered from below the street level; see L. Bosio, "Lapis in capite decussatus," *Memorie Storiche Forogiuliesi* 46, 1965, p. 5. Very likely this pillar also had a purely technical function.

[20] J. Bradford, *Ancient Landscapes*, p. 225; photographs and subsequent interpretations have been published by F. Castagnoli, "La Pianta di Metaponto," *Rend. Linc.* series 8, 14, 1959, p. 49; and by G. Schmiedt and R. Chevallier, "Caulonia e Metaponto," *L'Universo*, 1959. The date I have proposed (before the beginning of the fifth century) has been changed to mid-fifth century by G. Lo Porto, *Not. scavi*, 1966, p. 139, n. 9; and by D. Adamesteanu, *Rev. Arch.*, 1967, p. 8. On the other hand, the date has been brought to the era during which Metaponto was founded by A. Giuliano, *Urbanistica*, p. 44; by M. Coppa, *Storia dell'urbanistica*, p. 1013; and by Manni Piraino, *Parola del Passato* 23, 1968, p. 430 (who places it at the end of the seventh or beginning of the sixth century at the latest).

is found at Cyrene[21] by the third quarter of the sixth century B.C.

Excavations at Imera[22] have uncovered rectangular blocks whose short sides measure 32 meters and are datable around the beginning of the fifth century.

The urban pattern of Selinus[23] (the date of which is not yet ascertainable) presents a uniform grid of about 30 x 90 meters.

The lower sector of Heraclea of Lucania,[24] founded in 433–432 B.C., follows a uniform pattern (mirrored this time also in the perimeter walls), with blocks of 55 by 175 meters, possibly subdivided again.

Excavations at Camarina[25] have singled out a rectangular block whose short side measures one actus. Its first appearance is traced to the first half of the fifth century.

Also lower Locri[26] presents a uniform grid pattern whose short sides measure one actus. We are still unable to give a date to the first establishment of the plan.[27]

p. 56. The Greek City

The characteristics of the Hippodamean city plan are not to be confused with the basic tendency toward regularity and uniformity in city planning. Some examples of this tendency were given on page 56, to which we must add that of the city of Smyrna of the seventh century.[28] Nor should the schematic subdivision of the residential sector by axes in a single direction as at Monte Casale (Casmene, end of the seventh century[29]) be considered Hippodamean. In this case we are dealing with a geometric subdivision of the terrain in an almost rigid, militaristic fashion and certainly not comparable to the Hippodamean grid. A comparison of greater value might be with the plan of the residential

---

[21] S. Stucchi, *Cirene 1957–1966*, Tripoli, 1967, p. 41.
[22] A. Adriani, *Kokalos* 13, 1967, p. 230 and Table 34; E. Joly, in *Himera I*, Rome 1970, p. 270.
[23] G. Schmiedt, *Kokalos* 3, 1957, p. 22.
[24] G. Schmiedt and R. Chevallier, *L'Universo*, 1959; L. Quilici, *Siris-Heraclea* (Forma Italiae), Rome, 1967, p. 174, Fig. 331; B. Neutsch, "Herakleiastudien," *Röm. Mitt. Ergh.* 11, 1967, passim (D. Adamesteanu, *ibid.*, p. 96).
[25] See P. Pelagatti, *Boll. d'Arte*, 1962, pp. 259, 262.
[26] See F. Castagnoli, *Arch. Class.* 15, 1963, p. 191 and Table 68.
[27] We may hope for specific research for Akrai, to determine precisely the planimetric system and its chronology. See D. Adamesteanu, *Xth Congress of the International Society for Photogrammetry*, Lisbon, 1964, p. 8; P. Pelagatti, *Boll. d'Arte* 51, 1966, p. 92. For Syracuse, see M. Coppa, *Storia dell'urbanistica*, p. 901.
[28] J. M. Cook, "Old Smyrna 1948–51," *Annual Brit. Sch. Athens*, 53–54, 1958–59, p. 14; for Vroulia, see also H. Drerup, *Arch. Anz.* 1964, c. 219.
[29] A. Di Vita, "Un contributo all'urbanistica greca di Sicilia: Casmene," *Atti VII Congr. Intern. Arch. Class.* 2, Rome, 1961, p. 69, and "Per l'architettura," p. 46. A similar layout is found at Monte Bubbonia (6th century B.C.); see P. Orlandini, *Kokalos* 8, 1962, p. 86 and Table 10, 2.

sector of Enkomi[30] dating from the thirteenth century B.C., characterized by a central axis onto which open numerous streets almost at right angles to it. These streets subdivide the city into uniform rectangular blocks whose short sides measure about 100 feet. This plan, like others of the Mycenaean, Mesopotamian, and Egyptian world,[31] is an instructive example of the urbanistic expressions from which there developed the Hippodamean plan.

The recently discovered plan of the acropolis of Zernaki Tepe[32] (in the region of the Van lake in Urartu) must be added to the precedents of the Hippodamean plan. The city is reconstructed according to a grid of squares with sides of one actus, bisected by an *ambitus*; two larger streets intersecting at the center determine an axial scheme. According to available evidence, the city dates to the eighth century.

The attempt by Wycherley to attribute to Hippodamus the plan layout of Rhodes has been rather unconvincing. The reference to the epithet μετεωρολόγος (see pp. 66, 72) will not be valid in its intended sense, for the term not only means astronomer but carries with it the far greater meaning of physicist and thinker.[33]

p. 66. Hippodamus of Miletus

The conception of the Italic and Etruscan city as being of sacral

p. 74. The Etruscan and Italic City

[30] See P. Dikaios, *Arch. Anz.* 1962, c. 3; and in *Enkomi* 3, Mainz am Rhein, 1959, Table 1.
[31] See A. Badawy, "La maison mitoyenne de plan uniforme dans l'Egypte pharaonique," *Bull. Faculty of Arts, Cairo Univ.*, 17, 1953; and "Orthogonal and Axial Town Planning in Egypt," *Zeitschr. für Ägyptische Sprache* 85, 1959, p. 1; and *A History of Egyptian Architecture*, Berkeley and Los Angeles, 1966, especially p. 37. See also J. Schmidt, "Strassen in altorientalischen Wohngebieten," *Bagdader Mitteil.* 3, 1964, p. 125. P. Lampl, *Cities and Planning in the Ancient Near East*, New York, 1968; B. Brentjes, "Zum Verhältnis von Dorf und Stadt in Altvorderasien," in *Wiss. Zeitschr. d.M. Luther Univers. Halle-Wittenberg*, 17, 1968, p. 9.
[32] See C. A. Burney and G. R. J. Lawson, *Anatolian Studies* 10, 1960, p. 177; C. Nylander, *Orientalia Suecana* 14–15, 1965–66, p. 152.
[33] R. E. Wycherley, "Hippodamus and Rhodes," *Historia* 13, 1964, p. 135. On the other hand, considering the diffusion of the Hippodamean plan as early as the sixth century B.C., we could reconsider the question of chronology from the opposite perspective. That is, we could attribute Piraeus not to the age of Pericles but to that of Themistocles, trusting to the testimony of *Schol. ad Arist. Eq.* 327 (See I. Lana "L'Utopia di Ippodamo di Mileto," extracted from *Rivista di filosofia* 40, 1949). We could perhaps even hypothesize that Hippodamus had nothing to do with Thurii; indeed, the attribution of Thurii to him is based on two arguments: a corrupted text by Hesychius σατυρικούς which was corrected by Valesius to Θουριακούς. Cultrera proposes Σαμιακούς. In fact, it is possible that there was confusion with Hippodamus of Thurii, a Pythagorean philosopher who is thought not to be the architect Hippodamus (see I. Lana, "I frammenti del Pseudo Ippodamo Pitagorico," *Rivista di filosofia* 40, 1949). It would seem that the only confirmed period of the activity of Hippodamus was that around 478 B.C. For Hippodamus himself, see also R. Martin, *Encicl. Univ. Arte* 7, 1958, c. 86; F. Castagnoli, *Encicl. Arte Antica* 4, 1961, p. 183. For Piraeus, see also C. T. Panagos, *Le Pirée*, Athens, 1968, p. 201. J. S. Boersma, *Athenian Building Policy from 561–0 to 405–4 B.C.*, Groningen 1970, p. 47, 124.

origin still enjoys undeserved respect;[34] Marzabotto, Roma quadrata,[35] and centuriation,[36] are considered examples.

p. 84. Greek Cities of the Fourth Century B.C. and of the Hellenistic Era

The popularity and widespread use enjoyed by the Hippodamean city plan after the fifth century is documented by many new studies. Many such cities embodied important new urbanistic principles, although we shall cite only the works concerning Cnidos,[37] Soluntum[38] (excavations have brought to light data that confirm its fourth-century origins), Tindari,[39] Lipari,[40] Alexandria,[41] and the Seleucid cities in Syria.[42] We must also consider cities such as Ephesus[43] (blocks of 140 by 140 or 140 by 280 feet) and Segesta[44] (of rectangular layout notwithstanding the topography) as belonging to this class, even though they have not been so considered heretofore. We further have in this category Morgantina,[45] a city of the fourth century B.C. whose blocks measure 37.50 by 62 meters; Heraclea Minoa,[46] fourth century, whose plan reveals several orthogonal elements; Caulonia,[47] fourth century, with parallel streets spaced at 55 meters; Lilybaeum,[48] perhaps of the third century B.C., with blocks of 1

[34] See for example W. Müller, *Die heilige Stadt*, Stuttgart, 1962; P. Lavedan, *Histoire de l'urbanisme: Antiquité*, 2nd ed., Paris 1966. See also the exhaustive critique by R. A. Staccioli, *Arch. Class.* 20, 1968, p. 141; R. Bloch, *Rev. Archeol.*, 1, 1967, p. 381; H. H. Scullard, *The Etruscan Cities and Rome*, London 1967, p. 75; R. Lambrechts, *Les inscriptions avec le mot 'tular' et le bornage étrusque* (Bibl. St. Etr. 4), Florence 1970, p. 81; and finally see the many writings on Marzabotto cited in note 19, p. 133.

[35] For further discussion and bibliography I refer the reader to *Arch. Class.* 16, 1964, p. 178. I maintain that Roma quadrata is a relatively late invention of the Romans, for they imagined primitive Rome to be similar to the quadripartite cities (*quadratae*) which they founded from the fourth century on.

[36] F. Castagnoli, *Arch. Class.* 20, 1968, p. 123. For a discussion of the necropolis of Orvieto see A. Boethius, in *Classical Studies in Honour of B. L. Ullman* 1, Rome, 1964, p. 5. G. A. Mansuelli, *Studi Etr.* 37, 1970, p. 3. According to M. Pallottino, *Studi Etr.* 30, 1962, p. 181, the ordering of certain segments of the necropolis of Cerveteri reflects the influences of Hippodamean planning practices.

[37] M. J. Mellink, *Amer. J. Arch.* 72, 1968, p. 137, Table 59.

[38] See V. Tusa, *Kokalos* 3, 1957, p. 80; 4, 1958, p. 154. A revised city plan appears in *Fasti Arch.* 14, 1959, Table A.

[39] F. Barreca, "Tindari dal 345 al 317 A.C.," in *Kokalos* 4, 1958, p. 145. It is in this context that we must place the city of Alesa because of clearly rectangular plan elements. See G. Carettoni, *Not. Scavi.* 1959, p. 294.

[40] L. Bernabò Brea, "Lipari in the IV Century B.C.," *Kokalos* 4, 1958, p. 119.

[41] A. Adriani, *Repertorio d'Arte dell'Egitto greco–romano*, Series C, I–II, Palermo, 1966, p. 22.

[42] J. Lauffray "L'urbanisme antique en proche Orient," *Acta Congressus Madvigiani* 4, Copenhagen 1958, p. 7. G. and J.-Ch. Balty, in *Apamée de Syrie*, Brussels 1969, p. 33.

[43] A. Bammer, *Oesterr. Jahresh.* 46, 1961, p. 136.

[44] V. Tusa, *Atti VII Congr. Int. Arch. Class.* 2, Rome, 1961, p. 40.

[45] R. Stillwell, *Amer. J. Arch.* 71, 1967, p. 246.

[46] G. Schmiedt, *Kokalos* 3, 1957, p. 25; E. De Miro, *Kokalos* 12, 1966, p. 221.

[47] G. Schmiedt and R. Chevallier, *L'Universo*, 1959; F. Castagnoli, *Arch. Class.* 15, 1963, p. 195.

[48] G. Schmiedt, *Kokalos* 9, 1963, p. 49.

by 3 and 1 by 4 actus; Utica;[49] Ptolemais,[50] from the second half of the third century B.C., with four πλατεῖαι transversed at right angles by two πλατεῖαι and numerous στενωποί to form blocks generally measuring 36 by 180 meters; and finally Seleucia on the Tigris,[51] characterized by an agglomeration around a central axis with an offset agora. The blocks are 144.70 by 72.35 meters, about 4 by 2 actus.

p. 96. Roman Cities

Among the Roman cities of Hippodamean plan with elongated blocks we can include the following: Teano,[52] roads spaced at 39 by 59 meters, datable toward the end of the fourth century B.C.; Volsini,[53] perhaps from the middle of the third century, with some blocks of 2 by 4 actus, others slightly more than 3 by 2 actus; Ferento[54] from approximately the same period as Volsini, with blocks of 35 by 55 meters; Graviscae[55] from 181 B.C., with blocks of 100 feet by 2 actus; Telesia[56] of the Sillian era, with blocks of 1 actus by 300 feet.

The abundant research and studies[57] concerning those Roman cities based on the intersection of two major axes (with quasi-

[49] A. Lézine, *Carthage. Utique*, Paris 1968, p. 82. Utica dates from the first century B.C., but the plan must be attributed to the third century (see *Kokalos* 9, p. 187), and the same conclusion is proposed for the plan of Carthage.

[50] C. H. Kraeling, *Ptolemais*, Chicago, 1962, p. 37. We are not sure whether to attribute to this era the plan of Tauchira in Cyrenaica (*ibid.* p. 43). This city presents a rectangular layout following a strong median axis, with blocks of 38 by 71 or 39.5 by 83 meters.

[51] G. Gullini, "Un contributo alla storia dell'urbanistica: Seleucia sul Tigri," *Mesopotamia* 2, 1967, p. 135. For the cities of the Chersoneso see the bibliography included in the contribution of C. M. Danoff, Pauly–Wissowa, *Realencyclopaedie*, Suppl. 9, 1962, c. 1104; E. Belin de Bellu, *Histoire des colonies grecques du littoral nord de la Mer Noire*, Leiden, 1965. An approximation inspired by the Hippodamean plan is to be seen in the layout of Seuthopolis, Thrace, founded at the end of the fourth century B.C.; see also D. P. Dimitrov, *Atti VII Congr. Int. Arch. Class.* 1, Rome, 1961, p. 379; C. M. Danoff, Pauly–Wissowa, *Realencyclopaedie*, Suppl. 9, 1962, c. 1370. Any influx or influence of the Hippodamean plan in Numantia is strongly negated by A. Balil, *Rev. Arch.* 1962, p. 211.

[52] W. Johannowsky, *Boll. d'Arte* 31, 1963, p. 131.

[53] A. Fioravanti, *St. Etr.* 31, 1963, Table 2; M. L. Rinaldi, *Studi Romagnoli* 13, 1964, p. 105; C. F. Giuliani, "Bolsena e Ferento," *Quaderni dell'Istituto di Topografia Antica dell'Università* di Roma 2, Rome, 1966, p. 61.

[54] Giuliani, "Bolsena e Ferento."

[55] L. Quilici, "Graviscae," *Quaderni Ist. Top. Ant.* 4, 1968, p. 107. About the plan of Faleri Novi, see J. Ward Perkins, *Papers Brit. Sch. Rome*, 25, 1957, p. 156. For Alba Fucens, see J. Mertens, *Atti VII Congr. Int. Arch. Class.* 2, Rome 1961, p. 283; and by the same author, *Alba Fucens I*, Brussels, 1969. According to Martens, the present plan dates only partly from the time of the founding of the colony. As for the plan of Carthage, it should perhaps be removed from the frame of Roman planning (see note 49 above).

[56] L. Quilici, "Telesia," *Quaderni Ist. Top. Ant.* 2, 1966, p. 85.

[57] The following citations are limited to research of a general nature: G. A. Mansuelli, "L'urbanistica della regione VIII," *Atti VII Congr. Int. Arch. Class.* 2, 1961, p. 325; and "Osservazioni sull'urbanistica antica della Cisalpina," *Gli archeologi italiani in onore di A. Maiuri*, Cava dei Tirreni, 1965, p. 225. L. Harmand, "Le rempart urbain dans les provinces occidentales," *Atti VII*

square blocks) which mark the imposition of a new Roman order and give rise to important and varied city plans will require a new synthesis and ordering to account for the chronology and the geographic setting.

Congr. 3, p. 195. I would also like to include several studies on particular cities as published in the *Quaderni dell'Istituto di Topografia Antica dell'Università di Roma* 1, Rome, 1964, as follows: C. F. Giuliani, on Aquino, p. 41; A. La Regina, on Venafro, p. 55, and on Peltuinum, p. 69. In Volume 2, 1966, see C. F. Giuliani on Fondi, p. 71; A. La Regina on Sulmona, p. 107. Regarding Aquileia, see also L. Bertacchi, *Not Scavi* 1965, Suppl. p. 1.

Aside from the works cited in *Conclusion*, we should also mention M. Beresford, *New Towns of the Middle Ages*, London 1967. For discussion and a bibliography on the grid plan cities of China beginning in the sixth century B.C., see J. Tyrwhitt, "The City of Ch'ang-an," *The Town Planning Review* 39, 1968, p. 21. It is noteworthy that in China we find the same rigorous criteria of orthogonal subdivision applied to the layout of the fields as well as to the towns (see also F. Castagnoli, *Le ricerche sui resti della centuriazione*, Roma 1958, p. 30). Such observations may help clarify and interpret similar phenomena occurring in the Greek world. See A. Wasowicz, "Plan miasta i plan zaplecza rolniczego kolonii greckiej," *Kwartalnik Historii Kultury Materialne* 15, 1967j, p. 743; *Atti del Settimo Convegno di studi sulla Magna Grecia*, Naples 1968, p. 195.